LIVING ECHOES

A Collection of Meditations
by
Retired Lutheran Pastors

Edited by Rev. Howard Sortland

Bible Banner Press • Minneapolis, Minnesota

LIVING ECHOES
A collection of Meditations
by Retired Lutheran Pastors

Scripture taken from the Holy Bible,
New Revised Standard Version© 1989
by the Division of Christian Education of the National Council
of Churches of Christ in the United States of America

Editor: Rev. Howard Sortland
Cover Art: Don Wallerstedt

Library of Congress Catalog Card No.
97-75651
ISBN 1-891-428-50 0

First Edition
Printed in the United States of America

ACKNOWLEDGEMENTS

This collection would not have come to fruition without the assistance of many people involved in its preparation.

I offer my sincere gratitude to Karelyn Anderson, President of The Lutheran Bible Institute of Minneapolis, for supervising the project and providing her editing skills.

Thanks to Janice Serstock for preparing the printed copy and to Doris Mai for her assistance in preparing the finished product.

Special thanks to Don Wallerstedt for enhancing this publication with his art work.

My appreciation to Dr. William Halverson for his invaluable technical assistance.

FORWARD

The College of Retired Clergy is an organization of retired Evangelical Lutheran Church of America ministers which meets four times each year for the purpose of Christian fellowship as well as intellectual and spiritual growth. The idea of putting together this publication venture came to me at one of our meetings as I listened to one of our fellow former pastors present an inspiring, powerful devotional message. I thought, "Here is a room filled with nearly one hundred such persons with a veritable treasure-house of many years of memories and moving experiences. Why not make this wonderful resource available to our wider Lutheran family?"

*"Lord, speak to me that I may speak, in **living echoes** of Thy tone . . ."* It is this kind of prayer that we silently lifted to God as we entered our pulpits each Sunday so that our words were not our own, but rather *Living Echoes* of His tone. Thus, the title for this collection of meditations.

We took the proposal for this publication to the Board of Directors of The Lutheran Bible Institute of Minneapolis for their approval, and they gave us an enthusiastic, "Yes!" Next, we contacted all the retired clergy of the Minneapolis and St. Paul Area Synods of the ELCA, the

Minnesota South District of LCMS and the Association of Free Lutheran Churches to invite them to share a devotional meditation for this publication. We are very gratified by the response of our contributors in submitting to us these warm and inspiring devotional messages. We pray that they will provide you and your family a rich addition to your devotional life.

Rev. Howard Sortland

TABLE OF CONTENTS

Author	Page

Author	Page

Author	Page

Author	Page

*Lord, speak to me that I may speak
In Living Echoes of your tone;
As you have sought, so let us seek
Your straying children, lost and lone.*

Amen.

A WITNESS

by Dr. Rolf E. Aaseng

"In the same way, let your light so shine before others, so that they may see your good works and give glory to your Father in heaven." Matthew 5:16.

Harold is retired. To keep active he carries out groceries at the local supermarket.

Harold is one of the most effective witnesses for Christ that I know. He doesn't hand out tracts or ask if you're saved. He just goes about his small service to people in a pleasant, cheerful way.

His friendly greeting, smile of recognition, cheerful loading up of your purchases and genuine interest in how things are going for you, make you hope he'll be on duty when you do your shopping.

If he discovers you are a believer, he will share his faith with you and encourage you in your faith. If someone elderly comments, "I'm okay, especially considering the alternative," he may respond, "Well, the alternative for someone my age isn't so bad."

Harold "brightens the corner" where he is, as the old song goes. And the angels rejoice.

PRAYER:

Dear Lord, help me to live in such a way that I may reflect at least some of your glory to others. Amen.

1

GOD'S CALL

by Chaplain James A. Almquist
(COL) USAR RET

"And behold, the Lord passed by and a great and strong wind rent the mountains . . .but the Lord was not in the wind; and after the wind an earthquake, but the Lord was not in the earthquake, and after the earthquake a fire, but the Lord was not in the fire, and after the fire a still small voice . . . I Kings 19:12b

The call of God came to Samuel quietly, during the night, while he was still a boy. God's call to Saul (Paul) was very dramatic, while he was on the road to Damascus to persecute Christians. Others have had dramatic experiences hearing the call of the Lord — but not everyone. My experience with hearing God's call has generally been similar to the experience of Elijah in I Kings. Although it may not seem dramatic, it has been life changing for me. Usually the voice is accompanied by a set of experiences which, in hindsight, are more than coincidental. One such experience changed the entire direction of my life and ministry.

While serving as a young soldier in the U.S. Army, I believed I was called into the Army Chaplaincy. Years of preparation: college, seminary, Army Chaplain School, and two years of parish experience followed. Now, as a First Lieutenant and assigned to a reserve unit, the time had finally arrived to go into active duty as an Army Chaplain! After submitting all my application papers for active duty and telling the senior pastor of the church where I had been serving as youth pastor that I would be leaving, I returned to Fort Hamilton, New York, for an advanced course at the Army Chaplain School. Only then was I told that the Army was presently over its quota in Lutheran chaplains, and I could not be taken into active duty at that time! I could not believe it!

I remember sitting on my footlocker with my head in my hands, bitterly crying in my heart . . . and then came that still small voice: *"I have chosen you, and not cast you off; fear not, for I am with you, be not dismayed, for I am your God." (Isaiah 41).* I know now, many years later, that it was not coincidental that another Lutheran Chaplain from Seattle came by just then and I explained what had happened. A strange bright look came into his eye and he said, "Jim, didn't you serve in the Army in Alaska, and aren't you a pilot?" I said, "Yes." Then he explained that his church district had been looking for a pastor to serve in Nome, Alaska, as a flying missionary. He said, "I think God is calling you to Alaska." I didn't agree at the moment. But, two months later, I was Pastor of Our Savior's Lutheran Church in Nome, and Superintendent of Alaska Eskimo Missions.

God calls, sometimes in dramatic ways, but just as often it is in that "still small voice," and through situations and experiences that are more than coincidental.

PRAYER:

Dear Lord, help us to keep our minds and hearts open to hear your "still small voice." Give us faith to see your hand at work in the events of our daily lives. In Christ's name.
Amen.

FAITH IS LIKE A COIN

by Dr. Marbury E. Anderson

"But as for you, man of God, shun all this: pursue righteousness, godliness, faith, love, endurance, gentleness. Fight the good fight of the faith; take hold of the eternal life to which you were called and for which you made the good confession in the presence of many witnesses."
I Timothy 6:11-12.

I'm a debtor to a book. The book is *The Mirror of Faith* by the Norwegian theologian Pontoppidan. This book came into my life at a point when I was wrestling with assurance of my salvation. Likely you, as I, have met those who insist that if you don't have assurance you really don't have faith and aren't a born-again Christian. When I came upon the Pontoppidan book I was confused. I was asking, "If I am uncertain and have doubt, does it mean I am cut off from Christ?" I was also asking, "Are the host of faithful church-going people who are reluctant to firmly declare certainty of their salvation a people who really aren't Christian?"

Pontoppidan, in *The Mirror of Faith*, proposes answers to these questions. He says that faith is like a coin. It has two sides. The one he calls the active side. By the active side he refers to faith as a constant, tenacious clinging to Christ as lord and savior of life. The other side of faith he calls the passive side. By the passive side he refers to the good feelings that come, feelings such as peace, joy, assurance, and happiness. Pontoppidan takes the position that the active side of faith is the vital side. It is the side with which we need to concern ourselves and which we need to cultivate. The passive side, he suggests, will come in God's good time. It ought not be the focus of our attention and action.

Pontoppidan rescued me from a lot of insecurity and uncertainty. He took me out of the dependence upon my feelings — feelings which can be so elusive and temperamental. Pontoppidan, concerning my faith in Christ, caused me to "fight the good fight of faith." He moved me to the truth of the gospel as revealed in the saving work of the savior. He released me from nebulous feelings about salvation to the mighty facts of God's action of grace to save.

PRAYER:

Lord God, thank you for the gift of faith. May my faith rest on the facts of Christ and his saving work rather than on the mere feelings which come and go in my life. Amen.

WALKING WITH GOD

by Rev. Oscar A. Anderson

"Enoch walked with God. . ." Genesis 5:24a.

In an exercise conscious age, much stress is put on walking. For oldsters it is the exercise of choice. Legs have been called our second heart.

Walking is a frequent metaphor in scripture and Enoch's walk pictures what life is intended to be like. God wants us to be his walkers. It is worth noting that Jesus was engaged in making the lame walk, which has more than physical implications.

Walking with God means partnership. There is a sturdy experience described in that sentimental song: "And he walks with me and he talks with me . . ." With him, "You'll never walk alone."

Walking with God means everyday practice. Walking with God requires the discipline of humility. "Walk humbly with your God." It requires the regimen of obedience. "Walk in his ways." It requires the habit of honesty. "Walk in the light." It requires the determination to trust. "Walk by faith and not by sight."

Walking with God means progress. I cannot walk and stand still. Enoch walked with God and toward him who finally took him. "O for a closer walk with God," getting to know him better. Then when "I walk through the valley of the shadow" I will not fear, for "you are (walking) with me."

My father was an Enoch for me. He was an early teacher at LBI and he loved to go for walks. But he became ill and could not walk for the last nine years of his life. Still, whether leaning on his sons, lying in a hospital bed or preaching and teaching from a wheelchair, he walked with God. Prayer, Bible study, and meditation were his strong legs of faith. He firmly believed that he would be physically restored to walking and that faith kept him going until God took him. On the other side the divine promise was fulfilled, "they shall walk with me." One crippled saint put it this way. "I cannot walk but I can learn to dance."

PRAYER:

Lord, when I find it hard to walk on the outside, grant me grace to walk and even to dance on the inside. Amen.

I BELIEVE IN MIRACLES

by Rev. Dr. William E. Berg

"So if anyone is in Christ, there is a new creation: everything old has passed away; see, everything has become new!" IICorinthians 5:17.

I believe in miracles. There have been many in my life, both of body and spirit. The first miracle was my *rebirth in Holy Baptism*. It was the beginning of my journey of costly discipleship. This miracle cost Jesus his life. It cost my parents years of prayer, self-giving concern, disciplined nurture; yes, even some tears. Through their prayers and the care of the body of Christ, the church, I came to the place of a conscious response to divine mercy and grace.

Another miracle in my journey of faith is *the miracle of the "call"*. Since my confirmation in 1924, I had been running from my Lord and his call. His call was to full surrender, and to the gospel ministry. Like Jonah, I found another ship to other destinations. Following graduation from college in 1932, I came home to find my father in a coma. During a six-hour vigil at his bedside before he died, the divine call was confirmed. I quit running and rationalizing. I surrendered to the Lord. I was ordained in 1937.

All Christians are called! It is *a miracle of grace*. (John 15:16)

Following twenty-eight years in inner-city parish ministry, and twenty-eight years in evangelistic work in our national church and in the International Christian Ashram movement, the last four years have witnessed still another miracle. I call it *the miracle of undying hope*. Following a four-year illness, my beautiful wife and life partner of fifty-five years left us for her eternal home. It is indeed a faith-enhancing experience to learn from Jesus and a loved one how to live for others, how to suffer victoriously and how to die in the Lord. It's a miracle. (Revelation 14:13).

Many years ago I sat in a large church listening to Dr. E. Stanley Jones. From 1943, when I started attending his Christian Ashrams, to 1973, when he died, he was my spiritual mentor. That night (as he lifted up Jesus and his cross with the power of the Holy Spirit), I was so moved that I said, "Amen!" in a loud and clear voice. Dr. Jones stopped in his sermon, looked at me and said, "All my life I have been looking for a shouting Lutheran. At last I have found one!.." [Ed.: Now that's *a miracle of faith*!!]

Indeed, we *have* something to shout about!

PRAYER:

Lord, we pray that all of your miracles of grace for us on our earthly journey may be a prelude to the ultimate miracle of coming back to Paradise Regained. We look forward to shouting eternal praises to you there, and to serving you day and night in your temple. Amen.

ALONE

by Rev. Earl H. Berndtson

"Now when Jesus heard this, he withdrew from there in a boat to a deserted place by himself. But when the crowds heard it, they followed him on foot from the towns." Matthew 14:13.

"Six days later, Jesus took with him Peter and James and his brother John and led them up a high mountain, by themselves." Matthew 17:1.

Jesus had heard about John and his death at the order of King Herod. He needed to be alone with his Father God to grieve for John, and to cope with his own future.

The ministry of Jesus was also most intensive with the crowds draining his strength, with no opportunity to renew himself. So taking with him his closest disciples he went up a mountain to be alone with God. There he received the word that recharged him. *"This is my Son, the Beloved, with him I am well pleased; listen to him."* Matthew 17:5b.

We as Christians also need these moments to be alone with our Lord. In my 76 years of life I've had a number of such periods of time where I needed to be alone with God. I'm particularly mindful of perhaps my first time where life was just too busy, too full, too complicated to bear it any longer.

It came to me in my 21st year. Thankfully I had Christian parents who recognized my need and arranged a time and place for me to be alone. That summer, 1941, I was a student at the University of Minnesota Summer School of Forestry at Itasca State Park. It was six weeks of very intensive study, field trips, homework plus KP duty, and constant association with students and staff. Competition was keen and demanded much.

Upon completion of the course, my parents made arrangements for me to spend the week of July 19-26, 1941, at Mt. Carmel Bible Camp, then owned by LBI. What a contrast to the fiercely competitive environment at the Forestry Camp! I was placed in a bunk house with four other young men. Meals were served in the dining room with waitresses to serve us. At the very first breakfast I was seated with the staff, including Dr. Samuel Miller.

I discovered and still rejoice that every aspect of Mt. Carmel, including relationships with the staff and fellow campers, the classes, the waterfront, sports activities, and free time focused upon Christ, the Christian faith, and living the Christian life. It was truly a time where all these factors worked together and combined to make it a mountaintop experience for me personally.

PRAYER:

Thank you, Lord, for offering me and all Christians mountaintop experiences where we can be alone with you. Help us all to recognize our need of this, to claim it, and to assist others likewise to experience it. Amen.

GOD CHOSE YOU

by Captain Arvid E. Bidne
CHC, USN RET

"You did not choose me but I chose you. And I appointed you to go and bear fruit, fruit that will last, so that the Father will give you whatever you ask him in my name."
John 15:16.

I was 19 years old. I don't remember the trip from San Diego to the Small Craft Training Center in San Pedro, California. One thing I do remember: that I was very happy to be finished with Boot Camp. There were over 10,000 men and women in Advanced Training at this base. I didn't know a soul. Where would I be assigned? What would I do? How long would I be here? If there was no longer the possibility of a Class A school or officers training because of a six-month hospitalization with rheumatic fever, then what? A ship? A base in the Pacific?

For some reason, I was selected for base security, the "Seaman Guard Unit." Soon I was quite familiar with the new surroundings. Gradually, new friends were made. One noonhour I noticed a sign in the mess hall. A new Bible study was beginning that day in the chapel. Only 15 minutes, and we were welcome to attend. I went! There were 12-15 people present. The chaplain's Bible study was on John 15. One verse hit me. *"You did not choose me, but I chose you and appointed you that you should go and bear fruit and that your fruit should abide."* That Word was for *me* that particular day. And it has always been so! In struggling through the call to the ministry years later, "that Word" was definitive as far as I was concerned. The possibility of law school was no longer an option. Again and again I have turned to this verse of scripture and I have heard Jesus say, *"You did not choose me, but I chose you and appointed you that you should go and bear fruit and that your fruit should abide."* Many times over the years — sometimes when I was tired, sometimes when things should have gone better, sometimes in retirement — those words still have power and those words still beckon me forward. This favorite word of scripture has power. And it is a blessing!

PRAYER:

Our Gracious God, we thank you for your Word which confronts us, leads us, and guides us to our eternal home. In Jesus' name, Amen.

GOD OPENS SOME DOORS
AND CLOSES OTHERS

by Rev. Dallas F. Blenkush

"I will lead the blind by a road they do not know, by paths they have not known I will guide them . . ." Isaiah 42:16.

It's true. We do not always know when God is guiding or where the Lord is leading. I was not a good prospect for the ministry. Growing up I had three loves: sports, girls, and beer. I was good at all three. I graduated forty-second in a class of sixty-five and went to college only because a coach was sure I could play football. He was wrong.

My social life almost prevented it, but I did graduate with a degree in education with a major in speech. I taught one year and then was drafted and stationed in Washington, D.C. My wife, Sharon, and I attended a Lutheran congregation. I was asked by the Couples Club to give an outdoor Easter sermon and was subsequently told, "Man, you should be a pastor."

For some strange reason I became restless about going back to teaching. Remembering the reaction of the Couples Club, Sharon said, "You could always enter the ministry." We laughed with great gusto and then there was silence.

I talked with our pastor, wondering about the "call" to ministry. He said it's often simply God opening some doors and closing others. "Look at your recent past," he said. "Have you had any experiences that allowed you to taste and see what the ministry might be?" He suggested that maybe God had been guiding me and I was not aware of it.

I did look at my past and the results were scary:

- Had God used my ego to get me to college to play football?

- Had God given me an ease at public speaking?

- Would my education degree be helpful in my teaching ministry?

- While teaching high school, why was I asked to lead my congregation's stewardship program?

- While in Washington, why was I asked to teach Sunday School, get involved in the shepherding ministry, preach an Easter sermon?

- I had, at one point, planned to drop out of college and take up boxing as a career until I was told by a professional that I was very good, but not good enough. God does close doors.

Had God been guiding my path? After thirty years in the ministry, I believe he had.

PRAYER:

Gracious God, we do not always know where we are walking and where the path is going. We thank you for your guidance. We ask that your Spirit empower us, that our life may glorify your name. Amen.

AWAITING CHRIST'S RETURN

by Rev. Roy R. Bloomquist

"The boundary lines have fallen for me in pleasant places; I have a goodly heritage." Psalm 16:6

That verse is very meaningful to me whenever I review my ministry over the years. I can apply the good fortune expressed in that psalm to my own ministry. To indicate that I do not want this to be any self-exaltation, I am frank to admit that I have lingering memories of some past failures and regrets. So I will join the writer of these hymn lines:

> *I look not back, God knows the fruitless efforts,*
> *The wasted hours, the sinning, the regrets;*
> *I leave them all with him who blots the record*
> *And graciously forgives and then forgets!*

There is a "positive" side to consider. I remember with gratitude how the Lord led me in spite of my shortcomings. Bear with me as I personalize this and review what I see as divine providence.

I felt the call to ministry early in life. Each time I heard a sermon I had a desire to preach. After ordination I was called to a parish in Michigan which was a memorable experience.

Then the Lord fulfilled my desire to have a teaching ministry and I joined the faculty of Lutheran Bible Institute in Minneapolis and later in Seattle. After a few years in the classroom at LBI, the Lord again fulfilled a latent desire in me with a call to the Psalm of Life radio ministry which I continued for 24 years. What a blessing that was for me!

While I continued the teaching ministry on the radio, I was also led to assume leadership at Mount Carmel Camp for a number of years.

I retired in 1985, but the Lord still provided another challenge for ministry. He put in my mind and heart the urgency to share the promise of " . . .*Our blessed hope, and the manifestation of the glory of our great God and Savior, Jesus Christ" (Titus 2:13)*. For the past 10 years I have been writing *The Encourager*.

Someday my allotted time on earth will be over, but I look forward to exploring more "pleasant places" in that world to come. Heaven will flourish with unlimited opportunities for ministry for all eternity. Until that day is fulfilled, my wife and I decided to leave a witness even after we are gone from this world. So we have a cemetery marker with these words engraved on the stone: *AWAITING CHRIST'S RETURN!*

Now I am hopeful that you will review your life and think about all of the pleasant places where the Lord has led you providentially. Together we will agree that we have a goodly heritage.

PRAYER:

Father in heaven, thank you for your faithful providence to lead us into pleasant places of ministry. Thank you for the personal satisfaction and the sense of fulfillment in what you have called us to do. Help us, Lord, to continue to bring glory and honor to our Lord Jesus Christ, in whose name we pray. Amen!

SPEAK, LORD

by Rev. Richard E. Boye

"In the year that King Uzziah died, I saw the Lord sitting on a throne, high and lofty; and the hem of his robe filled the temple." Isaiah 6:1.

Shortly before I retired I went into the nave of the church I was serving one day to spend some quiet moments with God. Like Isaiah, I felt the presence of the Lord filling the sanctuary as one silent sermon after another came to me. My prayerful response was that of young Samuel which is printed on the next page.

My eyes first fastened on the Star of Bethlehem which hangs in the front of the church during the Epiphany season. I remembered how that Star led the Wise Men to "the place where the Child was." When they arrived, "They fell down and worshipped him." *I thus heard a message in the symbolism of the church when no one was speaking.*

Next, I focused on the large cross which hangs prominently at the front of the nave. It casts its shadow, as it were, upon the manger scene depicted in one of the stained glass windows. I thought again of God's eternal plan of salvation which centers in that cross. In St. Paul's words, "God shows his love for us in that while we were yet sinners Christ died for us." *The symbolism that surrounded me that day once again broke into silent speech.*

Then my attention was drawn to the window in the church where the Risen Christ is portrayed amid the lilies. It reminded me of his triumphant resurrection and his reassuring words, "I am the resurrection and the life. Those who believe in me, even though they die, will live, and everyone who lives and believes in me will never die." *Still another silent sermon was preached.*

Turning around, my gaze was lifted up to the large balcony window with its seven-fold tongues of fire enfolding the figure of Christ. I thought of Pentecost and the outpouring of the Holy Spirit; I thought also of that sermon which Peter could not hold in. I also remembered that the Bible says,
". . . no one can say 'Jesus is Lord' except by the Holy Spirit." *And thus through the beauty of symbolism still another powerful message reached my soul.*

PRAYER:

Speak, Lord, for your servant is listening. Amen.

THE PASSING OF A SAINT

by Rev. Thomas R. Boyer

"Precious in the sight of the Lord is the death of his faithful ones." Psalm 118:15

Late Saturday afternoon I was finishing my sermon preparation for the following morning when the phone rang and I was informed that Chris, a 95-year-old man, was not doing well. The nursing home was nine miles away, and since I had recently visited Chris I felt no need to go immediately. And so, I finished my tasks.

Following supper, my wife and I drove to the nursing home where we found Chris sitting up in bed, looking well and quite alert, surrounded by several family members who had cared for him for many years. Chris was a nice looking man (which belied his age) and was almost totally deaf. On my pastoral visits,when reading scripture, praying, sharing communion or simply conversing, I needed to speak in an extremely loud voice. This caused me some discomfort for I'm sure I was heard at great distances while sharing this special, private time.

Chris greeted me as we entered his room and I concluded his condition was not at all as serious as I had been told. I conversed briefly with Chris and family members and left to visit two other parishioners down the hall.

Returning to Chris' room, I found no change. I proceeded to have devotions (scripture and prayer) and conversation, thinking all the while that if we left and Chris had a good night's sleep, he would awaken refreshed and ready for another day.

Then, Chris spoke and thanked each family member for their kind and loving care given to him in the past years. I thought this was melodramatic, but said nothing. All was quiet in the room. We stood in silence. Then Chris spoke again, saying "It won't be long now." Again, moments of silence. Then Chris closed his eyes and breathed his last — his body at rest — his spirit at peace — his kindly face still and calm. I was speechless! All of us were speechless! Some wept softly. The nurse was informed and she came and covered that beautiful, peaceful face with a sheet — much too soon. We were in awe. I was inexperienced in this situation (this was my first church), yet I saw no reason to cover that peaceful face.

I can see him yet as I write and thank him for his living faith and beautiful death. As a child of just nine years of age, my own mother's death left me with strong negative thoughts of death and dying. Chris, that night, quietly and beautifully, full of faith and full of years, helped me to find something deep and blessed in the passing of a saint.

PRAYER:

We thank you, Lord, for the blessed memories of saints we have known and loved and who now rest from earthly labors — yet partake in the joys of your eternal kingdom. Amen.

SPREADING THE GOSPEL

by Rev. Roland C. Brandt

"Go therefore and make disciples of all nations." Matthew 28:19a.

The Highlands area of Papua, New Guinea, was a very fertile Lutheran mission field for a few decades after the end of World War II. A growing staff of overseas missionaries and national mission workers rejoiced at the large classes that were being instructed, baptized and organized into new Christian congregations. The baptisms of these large classes — often numbering in the hundreds — were huge, happy festivals. Large crowds of visitors, many of whom were Christian and many who were still in instruction classes, came from surrounding villages.

Dramatization of a selected Bible passage was usually a part of the festival. At one festival for our circuit in the Simbu province, the selected Bible passage was Ephesians 2:1-2a, 5: *"You were dead through the trespasses and sins in which you once lived, following the course of this world . . . even when we were dead through our trespasses, made us alive together with Christ — by grace you have been saved . . ."*

To dramatize this passage, a group of men dressed in their old garb and carried heavy loads of sticks and stones on their backs. These loads represented the burden of sin which they had to carry in the time before the coming of the gospel to their area. They struggled along with the heavy burdens for a short time, and then they all collapsed and fell down and lay on the ground as if they were dead — "dead through the trespasses and sins in which they once walked." While they were lying as though they were dead, an evangelist carrying a large wooden cross, dancing to the beat of drums, circled around them. This represented the proclamation of the gospel. The word for Good News in the local language is "miti." The miti was what revived them — "God made us alive!" Then they all stood up and the cross which the evangelist had carried was ceremoniously carried up a ladder and put in its place on the ridge pole of the newly constructed church.

This dramatization spoke powerfully to the mostly illiterate villagers, and helped them to understand what accepting and believing the gospel message would mean in their lives.

PRAYER:

Lord of the Church, may the gospel message continue to give us light and strength and enable us to participate in the work of spreading the gospel into all the world. Amen.

SHARE THE GOOD NEWS

by Rev. Harold C. Braun

"Jesus said, 'Let the little children come to me, and do not stop them; for it is to such as these that the kingdom of heaven belongs.'" Matthew 19:14.

It seemed like such a sad story. An eight-year-old son of delinquent rural parents lost a hand, cut off at the wrist when he fell from a moving harvest machine. I found the little red-headed, freckle-faced lad in the local hospital. He was so intensely interested as I told him the story of Jesus and our salvation. He was ready for more. It was all new to him. I also taught him how to pray, and the Lord's Prayer.

As I left the room, the attending nurse asked me to see a ten-year-old boy in an adjoining room, who was dying. But his irreligious and unbelieving father would not let me visit his son. You can imagine my dejected feeling as I left that small hospital. Had Satan won another victory? Another lost son?

The next day when I returned to visit my young friend, the nurse met me with a huge smile on her face. After I left the hospital, the nurses had moved the bed of my red-headed freckle-faced lad into the room of the dying son. He had heard the good news! He shared it with joy! He also taught him the prayers he had learned. Another soul rescued for Jesus.

What a powerful force the Gospel is! Whether we're young or old, let's make use of every opportunity to share it.

PRAYER:

*Gracious God, Father of Jesus Christ, our Lord and savior,
give us grateful hearts and the will to share the message of
salvation with everyone, young and old, as long as we have
life and breath. In Jesus' name we pray. Amen.*

AND I BECAME A POET

by Rev. Herbert F. Brokering

"For I am not ashamed of the gospel; it is the power of God for salvation to everyone who has faith, to the Jew first and also to the Greek." Romans 1:16.

In me lives a day to remember. Two days after Christmas my brother fell from a *willow* on a creek of *winter* ice. That day sixty-two years ago I became a poet; on a Sunday my nine years were compressed into a moment of passion, emotion, rhythm, beauty, inspiration. These are words in Webster to describe "poem." That Sunday, words began to rhyme — *wood, winter, willow, wonder, why, when, word*. I borrowed a Bible verse carved into an old gravestone next to Paul's new grave. The Word of God was proclaimed in red marble: "I am not ashamed of the gospel of Christ for it is the power of God unto salvation to all who believe." In our country church school, I chose a window seat to watch the grave. If Easter came soon I wanted a front row seat. I still sit at a window, watching and believing God's Word.

In Spring we planted Rose Moss on the grave. That year cement grave vaults came to our country cemetery, vaults insured for years and years. I believed they were not stronger than Easter and resurrection. but they were airtight — that's what I heard — but not resurrection proof.

The graves faced East and I knew why. When the dead in Nebraska would rise, they'd sit up, then stand — facing the Holy City. We sang "Jerusalem the Golden" in the white country church. At nine, I was sure the Golden City would be even more beautiful than the Nebraska State Capitol. It was a glad picture in me.

The feeling in me is not gone. I still write about water, wood, willow, weeping, wonder, watch, word, why. In 1935 these words churned like Lake Superior ice reshaping in late winter. I drew. With soft pencil I drew Joe Louis, world boxing champion. I drew ships in waves and deer scaling high fences. In my imagination I went beyond the country parsonage into God's world where ships sail, deer leap and Joe Louis wins. These I felt and drew. My favorite Bible verse was carved in marble on Pastor Geyer's gravestone, next to Paul, my brother. I borrowed the tombstone by leaning at the window, seeing, believing. God was saving my imagination.

I cannot imagine my life without that day when I was nine. Christmas and Easter met a Bible verse in marble — saved my world and I became a poet.

PRAYER:

O God of life, compress hard times into holy memory — through my believing in Jesus Christ. Amen.

FEEDING BODY AND SPIRIT

by Rev. L. David Brown

" . . . Blessed are you who are poor, for yours is the kingdom of God. Blessed are you who are hungry now, for you will be filled." Luke 6: 20-21.

In 1961 I was named to be a part of the delegation of the American Lutheran Church to the World Council of Churches Assembly in New Delhi, India. I believe I was the youngest delegate present, being in my early thirties. I had been in the U.S. Navy and had seen slums in many places in America, but was not prepared to witness the poverty I experienced in India. I could hardly comprehend the extent of such abject poverty as I saw there. Upon returning to America, I found it difficult to convey my experience of such hopelessness. I nearly came to the point of surrendering my ordination papers and seeking a job where I could make a difference in the two-thirds world of Asia, Africa and Latin America.

At that time, I was working in the youth office of the ALC. Though world hunger was hardly spoken of then, I began to speak of it everywhere I went. One person introduced me as the "Hunger Nut of the Lutheran Church." That appellation sort of stuck with me. Perhaps youth were the best audience to hear this word as one can almost see them attacked by the pangs of hunger when it comes to meal time. They proved to be good listeners, while adults paid little attention.

Luke gives us the beatitude that speaks of the poor and the hungry, unlike Matthew who speaks of the "poor in spirit" and those hungering "for righteousness." I believe Luke has it right. Jesus did not separate the body and the soul as we do in the Western world. Most older cultures do not divide these entities either, in this or other scripture.

As I write this devotional the world is laying Mother Theresa to rest. She cared for the physical bodies of the poorest of the poor, but no one would say of her that she has not been a spiritual force in this world. She would say, "As you look into the eyes of the poor, you can see Jesus." That is our call in this age of opulence in our country. For the way we treat the poor is a measure of our concern for the spiritual condition of other human beings.

PRAYER:

God, give us the grace to nourish the body and spirit of those lives we touch in our daily walk with you. Amen.

ALL IS OF GRACE

by Rev. David J. Campbell

". . . 'My grace is sufficient for you, for power is made perfect in weakness.'" 2 Corinthians 12:9

Such is the building and sustaining of Christian ministry — All is of God! This is the promise and power. This was my assurance through the years of my ministry — God's grace, all-sufficient.

There were two significant examples in my ministry in the area of church support. In my first parish, three small churches, sixty families in all, were left on their own when the fourth church of considerable size went on its own. The three churches then received mission aid. This was with great hesitation from the members of these churches. However, when the short-term aid ran out, it was possible by God's grace to lead them, by faith, to assume full self-sufficiency.

The second example was found with the last parish that I served. Suggestions for new programs to meet the needs of the congregation were often met with, "But we still owe on the church!" By God's grace alone they were led by a faithful God-fearing response of, "Let's pay it off." Before the church debt was totally paid off, the church members decided to embark on a new era with the United Mission Appeal, once again responding to God's grace with faith.

Important as church support is in its undergirding of Ministry, most treasured are the spiritual blessings realized in my ministry by God's grace. There was the PTR (Preaching, Teaching, Reaching) mission in my first parish with Pastor C. M. Hanson as our guest. The response to his message was a wonderful gospel outreach by God's grace.

In my second parish, God's grace opened the way to significant increases in the town and country churches' membership through visitation and personal witness. My own life was enriched at Mt. Carmel, formerly owned by LBI, as I spent time with Pastor Oscar Hanson. My next parish had no background in special meetings. Two meetings were held called "Life and Growth" to promote the gospel, by God's grace.

In my last parish, by God's grace we had a few families open their homes to Bible Studies. These small groups through prayer and dedication, led a week of special meetings that were led by Pastor Phillip Hanson. The reception was phenomenal.

In each parish the importance was on family ministry and missions. We were, by God's grace, concerned especially with regard to children, youth and adults to build faith and fellowship to his glory.

Over all, the words of our text proved true. "My grace is all you need, for my power is the greatest when you are weak." Through ministerial and personal life experiences, God's grace is constant and unfailing. In our faith and fellowship with God, Christian friends and associates, we cannot fail for "All is of God."

"Marvelous, infinite matchless grace. Freely bestowed on all who believe, you that are longing to see his face, will you this moment his Grace receive." Julia H. Johnston

PRAYER:

Dear Lord, thank you for the gift of your grace. While we wait to see you face to face, grant that we will live this moment in your grace. Amen.
JESUS' PROMISED PRESENCE

GIVES PEACE

by Rev. E. Roald Carlson

" . . . And remember, I am with you always, to the end of the age."   Matthew 28:20.

My parents were Lutheran missionaries in south Madagascar. Missionary children attended an American Mission School in a larger town called Fort Dauphin. When we made the two-day journey up the coast to spend vacation with our parents, we had to stay overnight at a village near the sea in a small house built by the French Colonial Government for travelers. It was primitive.

My father, who had come to get my two brothers and me, cooked supper on a Primus kerosene stove while we boys set up camp cots. Our father hung mosquito netting from the rafters to cover the cots.

After we crawled under the mosquito netting and got onto our camp cots, our father would carefully tuck the netting around the cots so that no malaria mosquitoes could enter. Then he would read a passage from the Bible, turn off the lantern, and crawl under his own mosquito netting. Next, he would pray a prayer for us, for our mother and our sister at the station in Manantenina and for a continued safe journey as we would ride one more day in palaquins carried on the
shoulders of four Malagasy men. After his "Amen," we
were all quiet.

Except that the noises of the night would now begin for us!
The wind . . . the roar of the ocean breakers . . . and the rats! The rats came out and ran around the floor

looking for any crumbs of food. Some ran along the rafters above our heads. I was glad for the mosquito netting that would at least keep them off me if they lost their footing up there.

For a small boy of six, it was frightening. I was tired, of course, and eventually went to sleep. But I remember how comforted I was by the presence of my father on his cot — just four feet away — and then the promised presence of Jesus. My father had specifically asked Jesus to stay beside us through the dark night, like a Good Shepherd, to watch over us. Gradually forgetting the terrors of the night, I went to sleep.

In my life I have found that for me, and for all Christians, Jesus is always there with us, just as He promised.

The winds blow, the ocean roars, the rats run about, the night is dark. Life is often hard, even cruel. Questions abound. The future is a puzzle. But with Jesus beside us, we can sleep in peace.

PRAYER:

O Lord, our Redeemer and Good Shepherd, stay with us always. Amen.

THE POWER OF PRAYER

by Rev. Roger E. Carlson

"Listen! I am standing at the door, knocking; if you hear my voice and open the door, I will come in to you and eat with you, and you with me." Revelation 3:20.

I'll never forget the encouragement to pray that Professor A. B. Anderson gave me when I attended LBI in South Minneapolis in the late 1930's. He began the study of prayer by saying, "The greatest weapon a Christian has is prayer. Even a child can pray so God can hear."

I remember a miraculous answer to prayer that occurred when I was in my first parish in Ft. Worth, Texas. A lady called me and she was crying. Her teenage son had been arrested and sentenced to the penitentiary for a year for riding in a stolen car with his friend. When the boy's friend was caught stealing another car, he confessed to the previous theft, naming the lady's son as an accomplice. I said I'd pray about the situation and she said she would too.

Having asked the lady the name of the judge handling the case, I called a Lutheran Brotherhood agent who had mentioned this judge in a speech. I asked him if he thought the judge would meet with me. "He's very serious," said the agent, "and will certainly ask why you didn't attend the trial. But I'll meet you in the courthouse lobby and when the judge returns from lunch you can get into the elevator and ride up to his office," he added.

The next day we waited in the lobby and when the judge came in the agent said, "There he is!" He looked like a football player! I got on the elevator, introduced myself, and referred to the teenager he had sentenced to prison. The judge abruptly said,

"Why didn't you attend the hearing? I don't change my decisions." I responded, "The mother was too ashamed to tell me."

By then we had reached the 7th floor and the judge invited me into his office to talk. I told the judge I felt the young man could be helped with counseling rather than prison. The judge then said if I would meet with the convicted teenager once a month, and send him a monthly typewritten report for one year, he would not send the boy to jail. "However, if you miss sending me even one report, off to jail he'll go!"

So, I met the boy and at our third meeting I asked him to accept Christ as his savior based on Revelation 3:20. He invited Jesus into his heart and began attending church regularly with his parents.

Two years later I resigned from my Texas congregation to accept a call to Madrid, Iowa. At the close of the program following the announcement of my resignation, the young man asked to say a few words. He had been working at a jewelry store and presented me a ring that had a silver cross and a small red jewel in the center. "I want to give this ring to Pastor Carlson because he helped me in a difficult situation," he said. "The cross stands for the cross where Jesus died for me and the red stone represents the blood he shed to wash away my sins."

I was so shocked, I nearly fainted. But I quickly realized that the change in this young man was God's answer to our prayers. Otherwise, the judge would not have changed his original decision to send the young man to prison.

PRAYER:

Thank you, dear God, for all the prayers you have heard and answered, for the wonderful blessings of your people. Amen.

GOD'S PERFECT TIMING

by Rev. Joan Conrad

"Proclaim the message; be persistent whether the time is favorable or unfavorable; convince, rebuke, and encourage, with the utmost patience in teaching." II Timothy 4:2.

From the day on which Christ Jesus himself saved me out of Mahayana Buddhism he never stopped changing my life. One recent event stands out.

It was very upsetting for me when, through unforeseeable circumstances, Mr. T. arrived so late for his appointment that it changed the schedule for my whole day. His offer of a ride after our session to my next destination made it seem more practical to visit a jail inmate immediately rather than later, as planned. Little did I know that this change of my schedule was to become the cure of my workaholism!

My inmate was a Native American with sky-blue eyes which his Norwegian grandmother had passed on to him, and which were the reason why he sometimes questioned his identity. Now he was sitting in his cell, reading the biography of "Murf the Surf," a convicted jewelry thief who became a Christian in a maximum security prison and had been instrumental in leading many prisoners to Christ. My inmate suddenly realized that Jesus was in prison, a death row inmate; that he knew what imprisonment is like and therefore understood how he, my prisoner, felt! Some kind of kinship developed in his mind which necessitated the question, "What would happen to me if I became a Christian, being a Native American?" He decided to pray that God would send him somebody with whom he could discuss this matter thoroughly.

His prayer received an instant answer when a guard came to lead him upstairs for "a religious visit."

God's timing is always perfect!

We talked for a long time in great depth, until we agreed that with Jesus he would not be less an American Indian, but he would rather, finally, become that man whom God wanted him to be.

As we prayed, the Holy Spirit took over and all of heaven rang with joy over the return of another repentant sinner to the Lord, who is serving his Lord in prison with the beautiful artistic talent which God gave him.

PRAYER:

Holy Triune God, Lord of my life with all its aspects, grant that I shall never set up a schedule without first asking that Your Will, not mine, be done — lest it interfere with Your perfect Will instead of bringing glory and honor to Your Holy Name. Amen.

GOD'S PLANS

by Rev. Lester A. Dahlen

"But seek the welfare of the city where I have sent you into exile, and pray to the Lord on its behalf, for in its welfare you will find your welfare." Jeremiah 29:7.

Though the original direction of God's words of exhortation were toward his children exiled in Babylon, they surely can and should apply to each of us in whatever our situation may be. The waves of refugees that swept out of China into Hong Kong following the 1949 Communist takeover of their homeland suggests one application of God's message to his people in Babylon.

Though many of them thought of Hong Kong as mainly a temporary city of refuge from which they eventually would move, others by choice (and some without choice) continued on in Hong Kong. Most of them found ways to stabilize their lives and in so doing, whether they realized it or not, were contributing to the welfare of their new community.

Christian congregations have also played important roles toward the welfare of Hong Kong. When the Koo family, Mandarin speaking refugees from the north, arrived in that largely Cantonese speaking city, they soon began searching for contact with people who spoke their dialect. Upon hearing that many who spoke their dialect were attending a certain Lutheran church where our family also worshipped and worked, the Koos visited and soon began to participate in the life of that Christian fellowship. Eventually they were baptized into Christ and his family.

There is no better way to contribute to the welfare of a community than to help its people become established in Christ. It is toward that goal that the congregations and seminary of the Evangelical Lutheran Church of Hong Kong have continued their ministry (which they also hoped would include China, from which many of them had fled earlier.)

Strange as it may seem, when Hong Kong is incorporated into China, the paths of many former refugees will have gone full circle. When that comes about, and many likely will experience difficulties, may they remember and cling to God's promise as recorded in Jeremiah 29:11: "I know the plans I have for you, plans for welfare and not for evil, to give you a future and a hope."

PRAYER:

Dear Lord, as we pray for the people of Hong Kong and China, help us also to pray for and seek the welfare of our own communities. Amen.

A WAITING SAVIOR

by Rev. Hubert DeBoer

"Listen! I am standing at the door, knocking; if you hear my voice and open the door, I will come in to you and eat with you, and you with me." Revelation 3:20.

Most everyone is familiar with the picture "The Light of the World" by Holman Hunt, illustrating Revelation 3:20. Christ stands with bowed head, listening. Vines have grown across the door, seemingly not having been opened for some time. The lantern's rays fall on some fruit which has dropped ungathered.

We see some of the infinite love of our savior, in that: though he is king of heaven and earth, yet he comes to us, not waiting for us to come to him! He stands at our heart's door as a supplicant. It is totally strange that we don't rush to throw open the door and welcome him in!

This isn't a picture of a prodigal son seeking the father, but greater love than that; the father seeking the prodigal! The question isn't, "Will the savior accept me?" No, the real question is: "Will I (we) REJECT the savior?"

Nor is the loving visitor satisfied simply to knock, for he calls, "If any man will hear my voice ..." Yes, he has spoken to multitudes and to individuals. He has never spoken a harsh word to any of us as he stood outside our heart's door. It is his voice of love which speaks volumes to the unyielding sinner, which says: "If any man hear my voice and opens the door, I will come in and sup with him and he with me."

When we go visiting, we are often very impatient. After a knock or two, having no response, we turn away. If we showed more perseverance, it might prove victorious for a soul that is seeking rest.

Even though we dilly-dally around before we open our heart's door, he won't break it down to gain entrance into our hearts. Scripture reads, in the last chapter of the Bible, "Whosoever will, let him drink of the water of life freely." *WHOSOEVER WILL*, having heard him, it remains for each individual to unbar the door of his own heart ... and let the Savior in! One of my Mom's favorite songs she often sang was, "There's a stranger at the door ... Let the Savior in."

PRAYER:

Thank you, Heavenly Father, for giving us such a savior who provides so abundantly for us. We needn't plan meals for him, but merely sup with him as he has brought his feast with him by the provisions on the cross. Nothing is lacking except guests for his banquet. Because of Jesus and his blood. Amen.

GUIDED MORALS
THE NEED OF THE DAY!

by Rev. Armin U. Deye

"For the grace of God has appeared, bringing salvation to all, training us to renounce impiety and worldly passions, and in the present age to live lives that are self-controlled, upright, and godly, . . ." Titus 2:11-12.

"We believe that human rebellion against God is at the core of the world's ills and that the crucifixion and resurrection of Jesus Christ represent God's ultimate response to human need, from which follows our Lord's call to, 'Love one another as I have loved you!' " These are the words of George Heider, President of Concordia University, River Forest, Illinois.

There are two main pedals in a car, the accelerator and the brake. It often thrills a driver to step on the gas pedal and zoom away, but if it were not for the brake pedal it would end tragically.

There is a similarity in our lives. Freedom appeals to the public in freedom of speech, freedom of morality, freedom of drugs and alcohol, etc. Live it up, step on the gas — that is the pedal of acceleration. Therefore, the brake pedal is so vital, yet often less attractive to the "driver." God knew that brakes would be so important to preserve the lives of people.
That is why he gave us the Ten Commandments. If we disregard the brake pedals of the "Thou shalts" and "Thou shalt nots" our lives will end in fatality.

Since there is a present-day movement to supplant "freedom of religion" to "freedom from religion" there has resulted a threatened tragedy. When God is eliminated from our schools and from our public life, it creates a vacuum. As soon as God and religion are eliminated the devil promptly moves in.

Christians must continue to be the "salt of the earth and the light of the world."

PRAYER:

Lord, grant us the conviction to fully accept you as the lord of heaven and earth, as the savior of all mankind and the courage to bear witness of your love and forgiveness for the salvation of people for eternity. In Jesus' name. Amen.

HONESTLY, WHAT DO WE REALLY WANT?

by Rev. Emmet E. Eklund

The Psalmist lists what we rightfully believe he considered to be the most precious of desires:

"Bless the Lord, O my soul, and all that is within me, bless his holy name. Bless the Lord, O my soul, and do not forget all his benefits — who forgives all your iniquity, who heals all your diseases, who redeems your life from the pit, who crowns you with steadfast love and mercy, who satisfies you with good as long as you live so that your youth is renewed like the eagle's." Psalm 103:1-5.

Do we have similar desires? The psalmist thanks God for forgiveness, healing from disease, redemption from eternal death, God's unfailing love and mercy.

On some points we agree: healing from disease and the gifts which sustain life. But what about forgiveness, redemption, love, and mercy? These can become second-class considerations as the example from our first ancestors tells us. Eve saw the forbidden fruit as *"good for food, . . . a delight to the eye, and . . . [could] make one wise."* Genesis 3:6. The infection of these priorities is still with us. Unlike the Psalmist, we would be sorely tempted to thank God for wealth which gives us what we consider necessary such as food and a great deal more, for pursuit of wisdom, and whatever is pleasing to us. These, however, leave unsatisfied our deepest needs as creatures created in his image. Pursuit of these possessions ends in anxieties.

Theologian Paul Tillich said that anxiety is the measure of our distance from God.

God's forgiveness, redemption, love and mercy alone give us that trust which removes these anxieties with their soul-eroding effects. God's word invites, *"Cast all your anxiety on him, because he cares for you."* I Peter 5:7.

By God's grace, we can become honest as the Psalmist was. In the crucified and risen Christ we are given these most precious gifts — forgiveness, redemption, love and mercy. With these blessings, there is no anxiety.

PRAYER:

Lord, empower us to desire the gifts which you desire for us that we may be rid of soul-destroying anxieties and know your peace which passes all understanding. Amen.

ENCOUNTER WITH JONES

by Rev. Dr. Lowell O. Erdahl,
Bishop Emeritus

"For in him all things in heaven and on earth were created, things visible and invisible, whether thrones or dominions or rulers or powers — all things have been created through him and for him. He himself is before all things, and in him all things hold together."   Colossians 1:16-17.

I sometimes wonder what my life would have been without my early encounter with E. Stanley Jones. His book, *The Way,* showed me that Christianity is not just a way of right belief and right behavior, but a way of living by the grace of God.

In addition to that fresh glimpse of grace, Jones gave me one of the central convictions of my life: I believe that the Christian way is the way we are created to live. That way, said Jones, is written "not only in the text of the Bible, but also in the texture of life." This is an awesome and exceedingly significant fact! Is it true that "all things have been created through Christ and for Christ" and that in Christ "all things hold together" (Colossians 1: 16, 17)? Are we created to live the life of trust and love that we see in Christ even as a fish is designed for the sea, a bird for the air, our eyes for sight, our ears for sound, a leaf for the sunshine? If that is true we had best be attentive to Jesus, for in him we see the person we are born to be and the life we are created to live!

We used to confess that "we are by nature sinful and unclean." I believe what that was trying to say, but not what it may seem to say. Our fallen nature is sinful, but that doesn't mean it's natural for us to sin and unnatural to live as we are created to live. "We have," as Jones liked to say, "been naturalized to the unnatural." We are so acclimated to sinful, self-centered living that we are like alcoholics who need detoxification and who go through painful withdrawal before experiencing joyful sobriety. Living with the self as god is not living as we are designed to live. In Christ, the death of the self as god is the birth of the self as an authentic human being. Then we live as we are created to live.

Jesus told Thomas, *"I am the way, and the truth, and the life. No one comes to the father except through me." (John 14:6).* That doesn't mean that only those who have correct theology concerning Jesus are welcomed by the Father. It means that God welcomes all who trust forgiving grace revealed and promised supremely in Jesus. Jesus not only said, *"I am the real and living way"* (Moffat's translation of *John 14:6*), but also *"Whoever believes in me believes not in me but in him who sent me. And whoever sees me sees him who sent me." (John 12:44, 45).* In Jesus we glimpse the heart of God and discover forgiving grace that welcomes us into the embrace of loving power and powerful love that receives and sustains us every moment. By that grace we live the *"life in fullness" (John 10:10)* that we are designed to live.

PRAYER:

We thank you, O Lord, for those life-changing encounters with your special servants like E. Stanley Jones. But even more, our encounter with you, O Christ — the Way, the Truth and the Life. Amen.

Some of this devotional has been adapted from my book, *Ten Habits for Effective Ministry: A Guide for Life-Giving Pastors*, Augsburg Fortress,1996.

LIVE WHAT YOU BELIEVE

by Rev. Leonard R. Flachman

*"But some one will say, 'You have faith and I have works.'
Show me your faith apart from your works, and I by my
works will show you my faith."* James 2:18.

Abdul was a powerful chieftain in the hot, barren
desert bordering the Red Sea on Ethiopia's east coast.
He reluctantly gave permission for a school to be built
and the children taught to read. His reluctance was
clearly articulated, "First you will teach our children
to read, then you will give them a Bible, then you will
change their faith." He further made his position
clear: "The day you bring a Bible into the school I
will kill you."

After the school was built, Abdul's son Mohammed
periodically appeared at our house early on a Sunday
morning. We would take him along to church. He
would sit quietly until the service was begun in "the
name of the Father, Son, and Holy Spirit." Offended
by our call on "three gods," Mohammed always
stalked out.

One Sunday morning, at the end of the rainy season,
Mohammed came to say that members of his tribe
had gotten into a shooting war with another tribe and
three of his "brothers" were wounded. He had been
to the provincial governor, the district governor, and
the provincial hospital seeking someone to go down
to the desert to bring the wounded back to the
hospital. No one else would help. Would we?

With no roads, it was a strenuous adventure in the
dry season to make the descent from the 7,000-foot
mountain elevation to the sea-level desert. At the end
of the rainy season the stream beds and valleys used

as "roads" had been blocked by boulders and fallen trees. With two landrovers, it took us three days to make the descent to the desert to find the wounded men.

The next Sunday, Mohammed appeared at our home to thank us. Again, we took him to church. He sat through the entire service. After the service, he accepted a Bible we gave him.

It was Abdul's son, Mohammed, who took the Bible into the desert village and had the children read it to him.

If we live what we believe, our witness is more profound.

PRAYER:

We pray, Lord, for a faith that shapes our lives, and for lives that reflect our faith. Amen.

A DIFFERENT KIND
OF THANKSGIVING

by Rev. Rodger N. Foltz

"Do not worry about anything, but in everything by prayer and supplication with thanksgiving let your requests be made known to God. And the peace of God, which surpasses all understanding, will guard your hearts and your minds in Christ Jesus." Philippians 4:6-7.

A precious pastor friend of mine used to say that of all the congregations he had served, one in particular was his "Philippian congregation," the congregation he remembered with special thanksgiving.

Paul had a special relationship with the Philippi congrega-tion. His letter breathes thanksgiving as he writes to the Philippian believers. He rejoices in remembering them (1:3). His letter is joyful throughout and devoted to positive teaching and friendly encouragement. Controversies and disputes do not occupy Paul's heart as he writes to his beloved friends at Philippi. They had been concerned about his privation (4:16). The hallmark of Paul's letter is joyful thanksgiving.

As we enjoy the brilliant, bright, beautiful autumn season, our senses are besieged by the bounty of harvest — pumpkin pies, mounds of mums, sheaves of cornstalks, and apple arrays have sprung up everywhere. We are made conscious of the plenty that we enjoy!

God would have us season our prayer life with thanksgiving "in everything." It is so easy for us to fall into a complain and blame mode in our lives, without even being aware of it. We need to be reminded and moved by God's Holy Spirit to praise him in every situation and thank him "in everything," because our flesh would have us do otherwise.

We are blessed to see how giving thanks "in everything" works itself out in the lives of God's people. Even as our senses are bombarded with the sights and smells of autumn, my mind is bombarded with the faces and voices of thankful believers:

John, who unceasingly praised God for the heart attack that limited his life to a few steps a day ... because he was, through it all, granted the grace to believe, and to live in the assurance of the forgiveness through the shed blood of Jesus.

The retired pastor couple, both beset by serious disease but full of enthusiasm for the simple joys of life arranged by God and possessed with a spirit of thankful service.

Mabel, dying of cancer, her body racked with pain, thanking God for his grace and goodness, and the way God used her disease and impending death to speak to her teenage children.

Ida, possessed of infirmity and stripped of health, possessions, and life-long friends in her old age, lifting up her feeble voice in joyous gratitude to the Lord.
And many, many more!

So marvelous are the lessons we learn from God's saints that the believer finds him/herself praying to God to do *whatever* he sees necessary for his/her good — no matter how uncomfortable it may be.

We rejoice with thanksgiving for God's *material gifts* of harvest and home, family and freedom. Sighs of

gratitude flow heavenward even more for the *grace* in Christ Jesus
which results in the peace of God guarding us, our hearts and minds. And as we walk with the Lord we even learn to give thanks for the unpleasant and uncomfortable things of life, which in God's hands produce a multitude of unanticipated and often temporarily hidden blessings in the lives of God's people.

PRAYER:

Dear Lord, grant us the grace of gratitude in everything and in all circumstances that all of our life is truly a thanks-giving.   Amen.

For the roses that I gather,
For the thorns their stems contain; Thanks for both, dear heav'nly Father,
Tho' the thorns have brought me pain. Thank you, God, that Thou dost give me
Peace and life eternally,
For these blessings on the journey
I will offer thanks to Thee!

Hymn: Thank You, Father, Stanza 4 — Geo. C. Stebbins

CONFESS CHRIST AS GOD

by Dr. Howard B. Franzen

" . . .Truly, this man was God's Son!" Matthew 27:54.

Having been a Chaplain in the United States Air Force for twenty-six years, active and reserve, I have a sensitivity for the man or woman in uniform. The text I have chosen points out the role of the Roman soldiers at the crucifixion of Jesus. They tend to be looked upon as the "bad guys" at the crucifixion.

They treated Jesus cruelly when he was in jail. They made him carry his cross. They nailed his hands and feet to the cross, then sat around gambling for his clothing while they waited for him to die. One of them rammed his lance into Jesus' side. Having stated his last words from the cross, Jesus cried with a loud voice and yielded up his spirit.

Before he died, the chief priests, watching Jesus on the cross, called out anything they thought would clinch the condemnation already upon Jesus. The most damning thing they could say was, ". . . he said, 'I am the son of God'!" Certainly the soldiers heard this accusation. What it meant to them then is hard to say.

Now these soldiers were Roman, and as such had religious beliefs. The Romans had many gods. The emperor was a god. The Roman was subject to magic, sorcery, superstition, demons and evil spirits. This would be true of these Roman soldiers. Their commander was called a centurion, meaning commander of one hundred men. The centurion ruled his men with an iron fist. Yet, the record of centurions in the New Testament shows them to have been men of quality and class.

When Jesus died on the cross, some amazing things began to take place. Among them was a terrible earthquake. Here was violence out of control! Imagine the feelings of those pagan soldiers and their commander. He would maintain discipline, but the factor that impressed the soldiers was in the earthquake. They would have thought of power, and who had ultimate power? No one but God! To them, God was angry because of what they had done to Jesus. Probably recalling the priest's statement, the soldiers concluded that this man must be the God's Son! So they said, "Truly, this was the Son of God!" And they meant it!

Have you made that claim? Have you declared to yourself, and to others, "Truly, Jesus is the Son of God and my savior!"

PRAYER:

Dear God, like the soldiers at the cross, may I repeat their confession. Amen.

THE PEACE OF GOD

by Rev. Wilbur C. Franzmeier

"And the peace of God, which transcends all understanding, will guard your hearts and your minds in Christ Jesus." Philippians 4:7.

This word of scripture has special meaning for me. A lady in a tuberculosis hospital made it come alive for me. As a seminary student we made hospital calls as part of our studies. Our class was assigned to a hospital treating TB patients. The lady who taught me had been a patient for 33 years. She could not leave her bed. She could not sit up over a 45-degree angle. She did much reading and needle work. Her husband had visited her once in these 33 years. She also knew she could not be cured by human efforts.

Our calls were made during the same time we had swimming privileges at the YMCA. This student was not happy about the situation. When I came to her bedside, I asked if I might read her a favorite portion of scripture. We talked, had a prayer and I went on to see other patients.

Over the weeks that our class made calls, my patient teacher seemed to sense my feeling that I would rather be swimming. She tried to cheer me, telling me how good God was to her. How much Jesus had done for her. She expressed her anticipation for the joys of heaven. She would reach out with her voice to cheer a fellow patient in the next bed who was despondent because she missed her family. She had been in the hospital for 9 years and within the year was going to be discharged.

It was some years before it dawned on me that she was indeed the one who ministered to me. She taught

me what it meant to have the "Peace of God" and how one lives the faith of victory. Hope is not a future event, but a *now* thing
that makes life sing.

This pastor still forgets and starts to feel sorry for himself. Then this little lady from 50 years ago reaches out with her quiet voice and calls me to rest in my Lord Jesus Christ.

PRAYER:

Dear Father, thank you for the special people who walk with you in the Light of your love and forgiveness. They put flesh and blood upon your promise for me in Jesus. By your grace, grant that someone may see your love in Christ for them through me. In Jesus' name. Amen.

THE HIGHEST RELATIONSHIP

by Rev. H. Daniel Friberg

"So we, who are many, are one body in Christ, and individually we are members of one another."
Romans 12:5.

By new birth, an individual is incorporated into the body of Christ and is made a member of that body. But this verse indicates a relationship not only of the believer to Christ but also of believers to one another. The foot provides mobility not only to itself, but also to the whole body. The eye provides vision not only to itself but also to the whole body.

Usually when one individual becomes alive in Christ by repentance and faith, his believing companions become aware of it. Recognizing it, they celebrate its occurrence. Our transcultural missionaries (I served several decades as such in China and Tanzania) have opportunity to see vividly the spiritual changes which can occur dramatically in people. At a gospel-declaring meeting in a church or marketplace, individuals or groups can be seen to be smitten in conscience and even, then and there, flooded with the joy of spiritual release. The idol-worshipper can, then and there, give up the worship of idols and lay hold on Christ as savior. The observing and perhaps ministering missionary then recognizes that a fundamental change has occurred. The converts may continually be greatly different from the missionary culturally, but in the most essential sense, he or she has become a brother or sister, child of God, and a precious member of Christ's body.

Headed for Jerusalem for the last time, Paul sent for the elders of the church in Ephesus to come to Miletus that he might say farewell to them before sailing on to

Palestine. When he announced that he would never see them again, these converted Gentiles and Jews, being deeply moved, wept freely and fell on Paul's neck and hugged him. Certainly he also hugged them in return in a dramatic manifestation of member-to-member endearment of Christ's true believers.

PRAYER:

Dear God, thank you for incorporating us as believers in Christ's body. Enable us by grace to exert ourselves faithfully for the multiplication of these body-members. Amen.

MEMBERS OF ONE BODY

by Rev. H. Daniel Friberg

"So we, who are many, are one body in Christ, and individually we are members of one another."
Romans 12:5.

I grew up in the home of a missionary doctor in central China. After studies in America, I returned to my native province of Honan and served as a cross-cultural missionary. Later I was sent to serve in East Africa.

The difference between our family and the people around us was considerable. It was of course cultural. China had a common written language and nearly every inland tribe of Africa had its own language and rule, illiterate until about a century ago. The Chinese were in fact a cultured nation a couple millennia before my ancestors in Sweden. The most significant difference, however, was in religion. Whereas we worship one true God, the Chinese worshipped exclusively image idols of metal, clay and wood; the African tribes wore and trusted in amulets and charms worn on the arms or neck.

A great change occurred with the entrance of the Gospel into these areas. I remember its dramatic power as it came into the hearts of people in revival meetings in the nineteen-thirties in central China and in the nineteen-forties in East Africa. Whatever cultural differences remained, the missionaries recognized the new converts as children of God and therefore completely brothers and sisters in Christ. So the whole community of believers, missionaries and nationals could say in the inspired words of Paul, "So we, being many, are one body in Christ, and individually members of one another." Despite the need of both missionaries and national or tribal converts to grow in trust and obedience to God, both could recognize in one another a blessed identity of character, members of God as our head and of one another as his spiritual creation and possessors of his life.

Let me add an incidental note: On my parents' last furlough from China my father arranged that I should be enrolled for one year, at age 15, in LBI which was then located in St.Paul, Minnesota, where the great Bible teacher, Dr. Samuel Miller, was one of my teachers.

PRAYER:

Dear Lord, we praise thee that thou hast chosen to create thyself a body consisting of all true believers in thy Son, Jesus Christ, as savior. Enable us who have been privileged to be incorporated into that body, by faith and testimony, to enlarge that body until the day that Christ lifts that body into the eternal bliss of heaven. Amen.

A CHOSEN FRIEND OF JESUS

by Rev. Ralph W. Glenn

"You did not choose me but I chose you. And I appointed you to go and bear fruit, fruit that will last, so that the Father will give you whatever you ask him in my name." John 15:16.

It is a wonderful thing to know that we are friends of Jesus. It is a wonderful thing to know that of all the things in life, we chose him. But it is even more wonderful to know that he chose us. Of all the people in the world that he could have chosen — of all the things in life that he could have had — he chose us.

I remember the time I was called out in the middle of the night to help an alcoholic woman. What a pitiful sight she was! And those around her were no better. There was, however, one woman who obviously didn't belong in that crowd. She was the one who spoke. "You may wonder why I am here," she said. Pointing to one of the women she said, "That woman is my daughter." Somewhat apologetically, she hastened on to say, "Well, she isn't really mine. I adopted her." For a moment there was an embarrassing silence, and then the words came tumbling out. "But that makes her all the more mine. Of all the little ones in the world, I chose her." Then, bursting into tears, she said, "But not for this. I didn't choose her for this. But I go with her whenever I can. I want to be there for her whenever she needs me. I keep hoping that I can win her away from all this."

And the thought comes to us. In like manner, Christ chose us. "But not for this." Not for what we have been or what we are. He chose us for what we can be in him. And he goes with us always — hoping to win us for himself.

He chose us, he says, so that we can go and bear fruit — the fruit of love, joy, peace . . . kindness, goodness . . . self-control — the fruit of the Spirit. He chose us to be witnesses wherever our steps may lead us.

It is a wonderful thing to know that we chose Jesus. But it is even more wonderful to know that of all the things in the world, he chose us. When this truth finally breaks in on our consciousness, it is as if a door has been thrown open to let the sunshine of God's love into our lives.

PRAYER:

Thank you, Lord, for choosing me. Amen.

THE GOOD WORD

by Rev. Kenneth Granquist

" . . .Why do you look for the living among the dead?"
Luke 24:5.

One Sunday after conducting a worship service at an out of town church, I stopped on the way home for a sandwich at a highway truck stop restaurant. All around the parking lot there were huge semi trucks, whose drivers were inside the restaurant eating their lunch.

Just before I finished eating my sandwich, a big, burly truck driver, dressed in a black jacket and boots, stopped at the table where I was seated. As I looked up, he said, "What's the good word, Parson?" He could see that I was a pastor by the clergy collar I was wearing.

He took me by surprise! I wasn't sure if he was joshing me, or testing me, or just making casual conversation. I mumbled something about the fact that it was the Easter season and that the Lord lives. He sat down at the table, and we began to talk. He was an over-the-road truck driver, hauling potatoes from Minnesota to Tennessee. His home is in a small town in Kentucky where he lives with his family. They regularly attend a small Assembly of God church. From his conversation I could tell that he was a lonely man who missed his wife and children and their way of life in that small town. And he was a Christian, having to make his way in an occupation that provides many temptations and obstacles to the Christian faith.

I think he really did want to hear some good word that day. He knew that the Lord lives. He just wanted someone else to say it.

The truck driver's question still haunts me. "What's the good word?" What is the good word for today, or for any day? Maybe my first stumbling response wasn't too far off the mark. We are always in the Easter mode. Jesus Christ *is* alive. He lives and promises life to us that is both abundant and eternal.

There are many people out there — moral people who care about their families and their church and their God. They do the best they can, sometimes in difficult situations. They, like we, need to hear the Good Word each day: The Lord lives!

PRAYER:

O Lord, help us to hear the Good Word, speak the Good Word, and live the Good Word of Jesus' resurrection. Amen.

TOWARD THE PERFECT DAY

by Rev. Harald D. Grindal

"But the path of the righteous is like the light of dawn, which shines brighter and brighter until full day."
Proverbs 4:18

What does it mean to be righteous? The text speaks of the "path of the righteous." Righteousness means to be right. This is the dictionary definition, but not the one implied by Scripture. When Scripture speaks about being righteous it means more than something human. In fact, the Bible declares that there is none righteous, none that doeth good, for all have gone utterly astray. How, then, can we be righteous? Simply this: We are righteous by faith in Christ who is our perfect righteousness. We sing it in the hymn, "My hope is built on nothing less/than Jesus' blood and righteousness/I dare not trust the sweetest frame,/but wholly lean on Jesus' name./On Christ the solid rock I stand./All other ground is sinking sand."

We must be sure that we are not standing before God in our own righteousness. For then we stand condemned, and lost, without hope. For our own righteousness is as filthy rags in the sight of our holy and righteous God.

It is only as we recognize that we are helpless and unworthy that God imputes his righteousness to us and forgives us. As we, through repentance and confession come to God, he accepts us as we are and covers our rags with the pure and lovely robe of Righteousness. This robe Christ provided for us by his death on the cross and by the perfect life he lived for us. How does this happen?

1) To be righteous is first to know that I have no righteousness of my own. 2) To be righteous is to have the righteousness of Christ by faith. 3) To be righteous is to walk in forgiveness every day. This is the paradox of the Christian faith. At the same time that I am declared righteous I am still a sinner. But as I daily trust Christ, then I know my sins are forgiven and I am walking the path of the righteous.

And what a path it is! It is like the dawning light. Have you watched the dawn? The glory of the sunrise as it fills the horizon with a golden glow. For a Christian who has been redeemed, life is a light which shines more and more until the perfect day. The perfect day, however, is never found here. It is the day which begins in heaven and continues forever. And the glory of the sunrise will be nothing like the glory that God has in store for his beloved children. But this path of the righteous leads through the valley of the shadow. For all of us, sooner or later, will come that lonely moment when alone, without human companionship, we must leave this world.

Here again we have the promise of God so we can say with the psalmist, "Yea, though I walk through the valley of the shadow of death I will fear no evil, for thou art with me, thy rod and thy staff they comfort me." Does the thought of death frighten you? It is quite natural. But remember that He will never leave you, his child. Bishop Bergraav told a story in one of his books about death. A father is taking his little son to the village miles away to get some supplies. They had to walk and on the way they crossed a narrow foot bridge over a rushing stream. It frightened the little boy. When they were on their way home he said to his father that he was afraid of crossing the bridge again. The father said, "Don't worry, son, I will carry you over the bridge." It was now dark and night had fallen. As the father carried his boy in his arms, the boy went to sleep and the father carried him over the bridge, into his home, and put him on his bed where he slept until the sun streamed in through the window the next morning. "This," says Bergraav, "is death for the Christian." We are fearful of the river we must cross alone and yet, our father takes us in his arms and carries us over. When we waken we are in the blaze of eternity's glory.

This is our assurance, that by faith and by grace we shall never be forsaken, for he will go with us all the way. Is this your hope, my friend? Do you know him, whom to know is life eternal?

As you remember those who have gone before, you may miss them, even as you thank God they were released from a life of pain and suffering. You may have many precious memories from their years with you. Now it may be time for you to cross that great river. Let the light of that perfect day draw you nearer to Christ, nearer to the home he has prepared for you. After all, we are but pilgrims and strangers here. As Mary Schindler wrote in her hymn about our pilgrimage,

"There the glory is ever shining;
O my longing heart, my longing heart is there.
Here in this country, so dark and dreary,
I long have wandered, forlorn and weary.
I'm a pilgrim, and I'm a stranger,
I can tarry, I can tarry but a night."

"Of that city to which I'm going
My Redeemer, my Redeemer is the light.
There is no sorrow, nor any sighing,
Nor any sinning, nor any dying.
Of that city to which I'm going
My Redeemer, my Redeemer is the light!"

PRAYER:

O dear Father, I thank you that you have promised through Jesus to take me in your arms, across the great river, into your bright and shining perfect day. Amen.

Editor's note: Pastor Harald Grindal passed away on May 26, 1997.

EVEN THROUGH OUR TEARS

by Rev. David F. Guenzel

*" . .Singing and making melody to the Lord in your hearts,
giving thanks to God the Father at all times and for
everything in the name of our Lord Jesus Christ."*
Ephesians 5:19b-20.

There he stood, second from the left in the front row
of little singers. All of five years old, he was scrubbed
clean with every blonde hair almost in place and the
white robe hanging as perfectly as it can on a wiggly
five-year-old.

The song began. Fifty little voices sang with great
enthusiasm, with one exception. The little cherub,
second from the left in the front row, was sobbing.
Big, uncontrollable sobs and teary cheeks caused the
white robe (almost as if by magic) to rise to that
cherubic face to stifle and dry.

But the sobs continued and so did the song. And then
on the chorus, through his tears, the little cherub
voiced the words he had learned: "Alleluia, I'll praise
the Lord!"

When life is happy, it's easy to praise the Lord. But
life has its tears, its hurts and separations, its
frustrations and anxieties. Sometimes we want to
hide or cover our faces. And we wonder if anyone
notices.

We want someone to notice. We want to get God's
attention. We are like the little boy who sat with his
family in the pizza shop. They were busy talking and
paying no particular attention to the little fellow.
Finally, in exasperation, he tugged on his dad's sleeve

and said in a voice that could not be ignored, "Look *to* me, Daddy!"

Look *to* us, God! Come to us, Jesus, in our smiles and in our tears. And into our awareness comes the promise, "I will be with you always, to the end of the age." Always, and in all things.

We hear the Psalmist in the 117th Psalm, *"Praise the Lord, all you peoples. For great is his steadfast love toward us, and the faithfulness of the Lord endures forever."*

The little cherub, second from the left, front row, reminds us that we can praise the Lord, even through our tears.

PRAYER:

O, God, for your loving presence in all the circumstances of life, we give you thanks. Help us to praise you when we laugh and as you hold us in your arms when we cry. In Jesus' name. Amen.

HE SURPRISES US WITH HIS LOVE

by Rev. Arndt L. Halvorson

"If we confess our sins, he is faithful and just to forgive us our sins, and cleanse us from all unrighteousness." I John 1:9.

Forgiveness is a "tough" word. The forgiven one often feels like he/she has had shock treatment while cleaning up unconfessed wrongs, and clearing up the confusion of his/her twisted mind.

In a teen-age group, a boy was asked if there had been any "clashes" in his group. His answer: "I'll say there were. It was a real 'happening.' We dug deep for forgiveness; we fought for survival; and some of us found Christian faith."

One of the fruits of "happening" has been the discovery of new words in telling the Good News. Martin Luther has given us many words to use in enjoying the gospel. He told his young son, "When we get to heaven, we will discover the word, 'surprise.' We will be *surprised* to see who did *not* get there; and we will be surprised to see who *did* get there!"

Surprise! It is strong medicine against cynicism. We should expect a radical surprise when the pastor declares the forgiveness of sins to me, a sinner. We are surprised when two ladies apologize and forgive one another. Work to be surprised! It may create a "Happening."

It happened in one of my early parishes. Two brothers and their sister lived together in an old, run-down house near the railroad tracks. We guessed they were old; they looked impoverished; their clothes were faded and ragged. We were told they were rich.

The older brother, a true miser, owned some buildings in the "red light district,"inhabited by prostitutes. He was certainly stingy. He didn't go to church because "all churches want is your money." But one Sunday, a surprise! He did come into a packed church, and sat in the front pew. When the offering was taken, he held a silver dollar high in the air for me to see. I made the victory sign and held up two fingers. Thinking I meant $2, he almost panicked as he vigorously shook his head "no." He had the call, but turned it down — no happening.

Meanwhile, the sister (who acted as their shepherdess) sent word to me that her younger brother was very ill, in the hospital. He was called the "dirty playboy." He was a reckless sort of fellow who had spent most of his energy in wrong ways. I went to see him but was the unwelcome guest. He rejected me at once with a loud curse and told me to leave. I felt defeated. I made a second call, was rejected; a third, likewise. On my fourth call, I found the young man in his bed, shut off by curtains. When I approached the bed I heard him talking. He was speaking in Norwegian. I could tell he was trying to remember the Lord's Prayer. He couldn't. He reached the sixth petition and stopped to sob, "Mor, Mor, jeg kan ikke huska." Mother, Mother, I can't remember! So I waited and he began again and fervently prayed until he reached that same point of not remembering. Then I joined him, in a loud voice.

"Og forlad os vor skjed, som og ir forlade vose skyldnere! Og led os ikke udi Fristelse men Frels os Fra det onde!" Forgive us our trespasses as we forgive those who trespass against us. And lead us not into temptation, but deliver us from evil.

He said, "Tak (Thanks)! My mother taught me to pray. We must do it again." A happening! And I said, "Let us pray:"

PRAYER:

Dear Lord, thank you for continuing to surprise us with your love. Strengthen humble servant girls like our sister in their ministry. Keep pushing your obstinate children toward the cross. In Jesus' name, Amen.

BAPTISM—OUR REAL BIRTHDAY

by Rev. Glen Hanggi

"So we do not lose heart. Even though our outer nature is wasting away, our inner nature is being renewed day by day." 2 Corinthians 4:16.

Perhaps I learned more about the meaning of baptism from our daughter than I learned in seminary. Kristen, our only daughter, was born on May 1 in Phoenix where I served as mission developer at Gloria Dei Lutheran Church. Since she was born just days before the formal organization of the congregation, she became, on May 21, both the first person to be baptized there and the first person I baptized after my ordination. For reasons unclear to me, Kris always remembered to celebrate her baptismal anniversary.

Twenty-one years later, on the eve of her birthday, Jan and I sat on the edge of her hospital bed and told her that it seemed her life was henceforth to be measured in weeks or months and not in years. At the end of her junior year of college, Kris presented the first symptoms of a rare, genetic liver disease. Ten weeks later she passed away.

From the Mayo Clinic we flew her to Pittsburgh, then to the Center for Liver Transplantation — but to no avail. When Jan arrived at her hospital room one morning, Kris greeted her by saying, "Mom, today's my baptismal day. We'll have to have a party!" A cupcake on her dinner tray provided the celebration.

Since the disease is very rare and seldom diagnosed before death, it seemed that every doctor wanted to examine this young nursing student. Because the disease was attacking the brain as well as the liver, the protocol for the examination usually began with a question, testing her cognitive functions. One day, about a week before she died, a doctor began his examination by asking, "Kris, when is your birthday?" Without a moment's pause, she replied, "May 21st, 196l." Jan and I were crushed; she couldn't even remember her birthday! Believing this to be the first signs of brain damage we had so dreaded, we left the room in tears. Only later did we realize what she had said. At that time, when only days remained for her — days filled with the worst kind of pain — when asked when she was born she responded more perceptively than we could at first understand. She said, "I was really born in my baptism."

It was at this same time that I read in our Sunday worship and later at her bedside these words from the Second Lesson: *"Even though our outer nature is wasting away, our inner nature is being renewed day by day." 2 Corinthians 4:16.*

PRAYER:

We thank you, our Heavenly Father, for the comforting realization that our loved one died being upheld by a deep and abiding faith in you. In Jesus' name. Amen.

WINSOME WITNESSES

by Dr. Edward A. Hansen
Bishop Emeritus

" . . .You will be my witnesses . . ." Acts 1:8.

To be a witness does not require a theological degree, or the taking of some courses in evangelism. One can witness with his lips, and also with his life, or manner of living. One can witness in ways that may seem very commonplace.

This truth was impressed upon me some years ago as I was taking the night train between New York and Detroit. As evening fell, I made my way through the rumbling coach cars to the diner, which appeared to be crowded with people chatting as they ate their evening meal. The steward said, "I don't have a private table left, but there is one place available at this table for four where I can seat you."

Nodding to the other three diners, I slipped into the vacant chair and was soon studying the menu. They were already engaged in animated conversation among themselves, which I could not help overhearing. I deduced that the man at my left was a doctor. Seated across the table were his wife and another woman, who may have been an aunt. Their conversation was becoming more animated.

Evidently they were returning from a medical convention, and the doctor's wife was saying, "I'm beginning to wonder if you think more of your medical meetings than you do of me. Tell me which you love most — your profession, or me?" The other lady murmured to the man, "You'd better not answer that, dearie!" "I guess not," the doctor said. "You never know what will happen when someone leads with the chin like that." The bemused look on my face must have been evident, as the doctor said, "We had better cut off this light conversation; this man over here is a clergyman."

Since I was not wearing any kind of clerical attire, I asked the man, "How do you know that?" "Well," he replied, "I don't know that, but this is the first time in my life that I have ever seen anyone bow his head and say grace for a meal in a dining car. So I came to the conclusion that you must be a man of God."

That remark opened the way to some continued conversation, in which I was able to say, among other things, that you don't have to be a clergyman to be thankful for daily food, or to invite the Lord Jesus to be your companion at meal time. It was a well-timed opportunity to be a witness.

"We are the only Bible

The careless world will read . . ."

PRAYER:

Heavenly Father, help us to be winsome witnesses to your grace and goodness wherever we go. For Jesus' sake. Amen.

THE CALL TO SERVICE

by Rev. Paul A. Hanson

"Jesus said . . . 'the Son of Man came not to be served, but to serve . . .'" Matthew 20:28

The church is the only societal structure this side of heaven which does not exist for itself. Its business, as the Body of Christ in this world, is to serve others.

Service, in Jesus' name, does not call attention to itself and is rendered in response to the love of the One who first loved us. It is, hopefully, a life style.

A powerful illustration of the nature of this call to service is provided by the work of the Youth Service Corps at the triennial Youth Gatherings held in the former American Lutheran Church and the current Evangelical Lutheran Church in America. These Gatherings, among the largest gatherings of high school age youth in this country, have served three generations of young people as instruments for equipping for mission and servant leadership.

Gathering logistics is challenging. Up to thirty-five thousand young people, coming from every state in the Union and abroad, accompanied by pastors, youth leaders, and counselors, need housing, food, and daily transportation to the host city's major convention center from up to fifty hotels (which have been "leased" for a five-day period.)

A sizeable Youth Service Corps is recruited for each Gathering to do the maintenance work, thus ensuring that participants will be freed to focus on having the best possible worship, learning, and "growing in faith" experience. The Corps' sole responsibility is to serve the needs of other Gathering participants. YSC members usually come from congregations located in or near the host city. They are "called" to *miss* the Gathering, even though present, in order that all others may attend.

The gift of their service in large measure makes possible the equipping for mission/leadership of all others in attendance. In so doing, they offer a "short course" in the meaning of Christian service for us all.

PRAYER:

Lord Jesus Christ, teach us to be your humble servants and to find our place in making the ministry of others possible. To that end, may Your will be done. We pray in Jesus' name. Amen.

EYES FIXED ON JESUS

by Rev. Rolf Hanson

"May I never boast of anything except the cross of our Lord Jesus Christ, by which the world has been crucified to me, and I to the world." Galatians 6:14.

Life is more than a cake walk, a bowl of cherries. Life is lived, as has been the case since Adam and Eve were expelled from Eden, confronted by two major ills called egomania and erotomania. The paths of life, the hymn writer says, are perplexing. A Welshman sings about a pilgrim traveling through a barren land. A Norwegian sings about folk who have come out of great tribulation. An African American man sings that nobody knows the trouble he has seen. I want to tell you about a great agony that is not in the song book.

A call came to my office from a farm house with the report that a fatal accident had occurred. As I drove into the farm yard, I saw the farmer's wife sitting on the grass cradling her dead husband in her arms. It was corn harvesting time and the farmer had been jacking up the front of one of his wagon boxes so the picked corn would be easier to unload. He was known as a careful man, a good farmer. A jack had slipped and crushed his head.

The harvest was to have been his last before retirement. He and his wife had been planning for years to make a trip or two and see some of the world beyond their county. In a split second their plans had been shattered. When I came up to the wife, she looked up and said, "Pastor, I see nothing ahead for me but the cross!" And then she said, what seemed like an after-thought, "but even God can do something about that."

She reminded me most emphatically that our ministry to one another in good times and in bad times is based solely on the forgiveness of sins assured for us in the death and resurrection of Jesus, the Christ.

The lady in this story, in spite of her tears and grief, was blessed with the ability to keep her eyes fixed on what Jesus had done for her, her husband, her kids — for all people. She would take up HER cross of suffering and grief because it was hers, and it was nothing to rejoice in — to glory in. She was able to say, however, with St. Paul, "I will *not* glory save *in the cross of our Lord Jesus Christ."*

She was old enough to be able to sing with assurance:

> "When through fiery trials your pathway shall lie,
> My grace, all sufficient, shall be your supply,
> The flames shall not hurt you; I only design
> Your dross to consume and your gold to refine."

PRAYER:

Lord Jesus Christ, you have redeemed us, lost and condemned creatures, bought and freed us from all sins, from death and the power of the devil. You have redeemed us not with silver and gold, but with your holy and precious blood, your innocent suffering and death. All that you have done that we might be your own, live under you in your Kingdom, and serve you in everlasting righteousness, innocence, and blessedness. Glory to you, O Christ. Amen.

VARIETY IS GOD'S GIFT

by Rev. William J. Hanson

"I have other sheep that do not belong to this fold. I must bring them also, and they will listen to my voice. So there will be one flock, one shepherd." John 10:16.

The spiritual emphasis in the Lutheran tradition in which I was raised was very personal. There was a strong focus on reaching a personal understanding about being a child of God through grace. It was healthy. This personal conviction and commitment was nurtured in one's own congregation. This group of concerned fellow Christians surrounded the individual with support, guidance and love.

The congregation was loosely affiliated with other congregations of like-minded people. This like-mindedness included a spiritual emphasis and a cultural homogeneity. The affiliation was necessary so as to accomplish things an individual or individual congregation could not do alone; i.e., train pastors, send missionaries or publish curricula. This emphasis was from the singular (the individual and/or congregation) to the plural (the church body).

As Lutheranism has experienced mergers, I have been thrown together with "other sheep not of this flock." What a shock! The shock wasn't simply due to differences in patterns of piety but in an understanding of the church. This was not a radical change but an awareness that the church has a life, given it by God, beyond me and my congregation.

I have grown because of the whole church. The scriptures are mine not because my congregation retained them, but because a wide variety of Christians have saved and shared them through the centuries. My Christian life is much richer because I have encountered women and men who have seen things differently than I do. My appreciation of liturgy has expanded because of a wider variety of traditions being a part of our worship life. Today, ministry is a larger concept than ever. The larger church isn't a threat but a variety of structures, histories, thoughts, ministries — all equal attempts to be faithful to God's will. The plural has become a way for God to enrich the singular, and what a blessing that has been!

There may be more growth for me in the future as my own ecumenical understanding and experience expands. I *know* there will be more when I get to heaven and enjoy the wide and rich variety of God's people.

PRAYER:

Thank you, Lord, for the richness we can enjoy as we grow through your word and through our expanding experiences with your people. Amen.

TIS MORE BLESSED TO GIVE
THAN TO RECEIVE

by Rev. Stanton R. Hecksel

" . . . remembering the words of the Lord Jesus, for he himself said, 'It is more blessed to give than to receive.'" Acts 20:35.

It was our son who really brought home the meaning of these words. He was a preschooler looking at pictures in the advertising section of the Sunday paper before Christmas, when he saw a gift he thought our family could use. He had his mother take him to the department store, wait nearby with her back turned away from him while he went off to make his purchase with the nickels, dimes and quarters he had saved up.

That Christmas he was thrilled with the toys and gifts he received. But his biggest thrill was to be able to give our family a gift that he had picked out all by himself and paid for by himself. That meant more to him than any of the gifts he had received. We've used the ice cream maker he gave us many times since then!

I've thought about that little incident many times. Certainly our greatest satisfaction and that good all-over feeling comes from giving rather than receiving. Even Jesus Christ, wracked as he was by the terribly indescribable pain of the cross, could pray, "Father, forgive them; for they know not what they do," as he prayed for you, me and all other human beings. The forgiveness we experience today and the hope of life everlasting living in our hearts and minds comes because Jesus Christ gave himself for us on the cross. One wonders how much satisfaction and contentment can be gained in receiving ultra-high bonuses while laying off a lot of people who live just one paycheck away from financial ruin.

Beyond a doubt, greed is giving in to the sinful impulses of our human nature. Giving is responding to the Holy Spirit's promptings and urgings. Not that receiving is wrong. Indeed not! After all, we need to give other people the joy of giving, too! But given the selfish nature of our sinful selves, we need not worry about that.

Rather, we need to learn the grace of giving, giving not just money and things, but ourselves, our time, the special skills God has implanted in all of us. All of it for the blessing and enjoyment of others. In the process, we'll find ourselves blessed beyond measure.

God grant us the grace of giving!

PRAYER:

Heavenly Father, you have given us more than we ever dared to dream of or hope for when you sent your Son, Jesus Christ, to bear our sin and give us an eternal hope. Grant that we may follow your example of giving, as imperfect as it will be, and learn the grace of giving. Through your Son, Jesus Christ our Lord, Amen.

PERMISSION TO BE HAPPY

by Rev. Walter G. Hed

"As a deer longs for flowing streams, so my soul longs for you, O God. My soul thirsts for God, for the living God. When shall I come and behold the face of God? Psalm 42: 1-2.

As a chaplain, I have worked in the field of chemical dependency for over 15 years. Typical chaplaincy involvement included some lectures and working with 2nd, 3rd, and 4th step groups as well as the very time-consuming 5th step work. Hundreds of 5th steps have convinced me that we, as human beings, have a tremendous ability to survive. I am often impressed with the fact that people go through what they do and live to talk about it. Although my own story would not be as critical as many that I've heard, I believe that I too am a survivor. We all are.

There is a difference, however, between *surviving* and *living*. Spirituality might be defined as going beyond survival to living. Based on my own experience and some reading, the following points might serve to define what it is to be alive — spiritually healthy.

1. Being AWARE. Having a sense of who we are. This may mean being aware of one's fears but not feeling trapped by them. Having a sense of self may mean avoiding the trap of believing life would be happier if our circumstances were different.

2. Being AUTHENTIC. We are more alive when we are not pretending to be someone we are not.   Being honest. Rather than wishing things were otherwise, develop and enjoy your existing strengths.

3. Being WILLING TO CHANGE. Pursue personal growth. We are more alive when we take advantage of learning everything possible from life. Pursue new truths. St. Augustine encourages us in this direction when he says, "Where I found truth, there I found God."

4. Being GENEROUS IN OUR LOVE. Spiritual health may ask that we be friends with select persons but it does not mean being a surrogate "mommy" or "daddy" to others. To love is to let others be what they were created to be and this means trusting God who is, after all, greater than we.

5. Having a SENSE OF HUMOR. Spiritually healthy people seem to have a sense of the tragic-comic nature of life. They are able to laugh at themselves. For most of us, this does not come easily. I am reminded of a Peanuts cartoon which shows Snoopy bouncing gleefully past Charlie Brown and Lucy. They are both disturbed about something. In the next frame, Lucy says, "Look at that crazy dog!" In the third frame, Charlie Brown says, "I sure wish I could be happy all the time." In the last frame, Lucy says, "Not me! It's hard to feel sorry for yourself when you're happy."

Giving ourselves permission to be happy is to risk going beyond survival to spirituality — which is living.

PRAYER:

Thank you, Lord, for the gift of spiritual health and for your peace. Amen.

RELIGION AND SPIRITUALITY

by Rev. Walter G. Hed

" . . . looking to Jesus the pioneer and perfecter of our faith,
who for the sake of the joy that was set before him endured
the cross, disregarding its shame, and has taken his seat at
the right hand of the throne of God." Hebrews 12:2.

What is the difference between religion and
spirituality? The answer I would give to this question
today is different from what I would have given 10-20
years ago.

Words I associate with "religion" include church,
dogma, clergy, liturgy, piety, [sometimes] hypocrisy,
structure, buildings, catechism, hymns, Sunday
School, the papacy, and offerings. I also think of
some special people who have had a positive
influence on my life. When I think of "spirituality",
building a list of associated terms becomes a little
more difficult. I think of serenity, peace, being
grateful, openness, prayer, trust and positiveness.
(You might wish to add to these lists based on your
own background and experience.)

You will notice that the words associated with *religion*
are more concrete or tangible than those associated
with *spirituality* , which is more illusive and difficult
to define. Maybe that is why it seems easier for a
person to "get into" religion than into spirituality.
Maybe it is possible for a person to have religion
without spirituality. Or, maybe it is possible for a
person to have spirituality without religion. Of
course, it is possible to have both. But the very nature
of spirituality seems to be that we cannot box it or
create it ourselves. It is a gift — a gift of relationship.
To have faith and trust in a power beyond ourselves
is the big break-through of spirituality. As has been
said, "It is when we dare to trust others that
redemptive transformation occurs."

The renowned theologian Paul Tillich says that faith is, "The state of being grasped by an ultimate concern." As he writes in Systematic Theology II 60, "Faith, as the Spiritual Presence's invasion of the conflicts and ambiguities of man's life under the dimension of the spirit, is not an act of cognitive affirmation within the subject-object structure of reality." In other words, faith or trust does not come to us through our own creative powers of the intellect or will. We as finite people cannot raise ourselves to become infinite. It is the other way around. The infinite grasps the finite. Since as human beings we cannot reach the ultimate, we need to be reached by it. As human beings we need to surrender to God so that our fantasies of being all-powerful ourselves can be given up. Self-centeredness can be put aside so that the true center of all existence might be given power over us.

For me, spirituality is life itself. And, it goes better when I surrender to Christ. Having listened to hundreds of 5th steps, I am absolutely impressed with the ability of the human being to survive. I know that I am a survivor too. But surviving is not the same as living. Living is accepting the truth about one's self and about one's situation. The need to assume power becomes less important because one views it from a whole new perspective when life is seen as a gift. The question now becomes, "What shall I do with the gift of life I have been given?" That's a new and exciting kind of power! With that clearly before me, I am free to choose — or not to choose — my form of religious expression.

PRAYER:

Dear Heavenly Father, we thank you for the gift of faith as we thank you for the gift of life. Help us to surrender our will to you and to be truly alive in your presence. Amen.

CHILD-LIKE FAITH

by Rev. Lester F. Heins

". . . Jesus said, 'Let the children come to me, and do not stop them; for it is to such as these that the kingdom of heaven belongs.'" Matthew 19:14.

Disciples of Jesus wanted to know who would be "greatest" in the kingdom of heaven about which they had been hearing him preach. *Lord, as we read and ponder and pray with the whole assembly of your church in worship, open our hearts to your enlightening message. May we all come to you in worship as children!*

The picture deepens and it perpetuates a mystery as we read. We can explain and exclaim; we can calculate and speculate. And finally the truth emerges. We must believe! It is in coming to believe this that we are "born again," whether consciously or otherwise.

Our faith is anchored in the physical reality of our human birth and the spiritual power of faith in our baptism. We are thereby set on the course that is promised through time into an inheritance that is beyond our natural capacity to believe or even to imagine. The three synoptic gospel records, Matthew, Mark and Luke, all include this important emphasis on what each of them has written for our spiritual nourishment.

Matthew is quoted as a text above.

Mark 9: 36-37: "Then he took a little child and put it among them; and taking it in his arms, he said to them, 'Whoever welcomes one such child in my name welcomes me, and whoever welcomes me welcomes not me but the one who sent me.'"

Luke 9:47-48: "But Jesus, aware of their inner thoughts, took a little child and put it by his side, and said to them, 'Whoever welcomes this child in my name welcomes me, and whoever welcomes me welcomes the one who sent me; for the least among all of you is the greatest.'"

PRAYER:

Enable us, Lord Jesus, to become as little children in our ability, not to understand, but to believe and to experience and to fully absorb the wonders of your love. Amen.

GOD'S WAYS AND OUR WAYS

by Rev. Lowell L. Hesterman

"For as the heavens are higher than the earth, so are my ways higher than your ways, and my thoughts than your thoughts." Isaiah 55:9.

As I flew across the Atlantic for about the twentieth time while traveling for the World Mission office, I recalled a time in the seminary when I had turned down an internship with the youth department. I declined because, as I said, "I don't like to travel." I could only smile at the way God's plans for us may differ from our own.

This reminded me of another bargain I thought I had made with the Lord. During my senior year, wondering about my first call in the ministry, I thought I was being generous when I prayed, "Lord, I'll go anywhere you want me to go, even to an overseas mission. However, I'd rather not go to a large city, but if that's necessary, please, not to a mission congregation."

My second call was to begin a new congregation in Dayton, Ohio. Perhaps the Lord smiled as I struggled with this decision. When I became convinced that it was the Lord's call, I accepted. Five tremendously exciting years followed as I had the privilege of meeting people searching for answers to life that could only be found in the Gospel of Jesus Christ.

God's plans for me were different from what I had anticipated. Looking back over four decades of ministry, I can't imagine a richer, more exciting, more demanding kind of ministry. God had planted surprises all along the way.

Things don't always go as we plan, expect, or hope in life. There are disappointments, setbacks,and perhaps adversities. When life takes an unexpected turn, we can open our hearts to God and let God speak to us through the Prophet Isaiah, "My ways are higher than your ways." Through the cross of Jesus, God has secured us in his love. Nothing can separate us from God. Through faith, we rest secure that God possesses our lives. His ways and thoughts are higher and better than ours. That is good news. Amen!

PRAYER:

Lord, grant us a rich measure of faith that we may eagerly follow your leading. In Jesus' name we pray. Amen.

BLESSING OBSERVED

by Rev. Vernon A. Hintermeyer

"Give thanks in all circumstances; for this is the will of God in Christ Jesus for you." I Thessalonians 5:18.

"Did you hear about George?" Word spread in the community, for its Chief of Police was in the hospital. With a concerned tone to their voices they added, "They say it's cancer."

His family members were active in church but he was usually busy and "didn't have time to spend an hour for worship." He was a good man. His concern for his city and those in it was genuine and dedicated. Now the family pastor stopped to ask, "How are you doing, George?"

The rumor was correct; it was cancer. His body grew weaker each day as he spent those weeks at home with family. The regular pastoral visits dealt with the realities of humanity, living and dying. It was a time for serious considerations about one's relationship with God. Now, his faith in the death, resurrection, and power of Jesus Christ had a new meaning to him.

A few visits later, George stated, "Pastor, I have been thanking God for this cancer. When I think of all the bodies I have helped pick up after accidents — times when they were killed without any warning, I thank God for giving me time to prepare for death. I have been thanking him for being with me and providing inner comfort." He added, "I hope others can learn from me that you need to be ready to meet God."

It is not always easy to give thanks "in" all circumstances, nor "for" all circumstances, but George had found a secret. God had given him time to prepare to die. Then, claiming the victory over death, he praised and thanked God for such a moment.

Are we thankful in our circumstances? Have we appreciated the many times we have been reminded of God's love? Are we ready to meet our loving merciful God? How much do we give thanks?

PRAYER:

Father in heaven, thank you for your love, your mercy, and the invitation to follow you by faith. Grant us a saving faith that we may be ready to meet you in death or at the return of Christ. Guide our life each day. In the name of Jesus, your Son, we pray. Amen.

WHAT'S AN ECHO?

by Rev. Vernon A. Hintermeyer

"This is the message we have heard from him and proclaim to you, that God is light and in him there is no darkness at all." I John 1:5.

It was after a Friday night basketball game in January. Eleven high school youth met in the parsonage to report on their adventures during the Christmas break. They had attended an exciting youth event but now wanted to share with their pastor a concern they had about their congregation. How could they relay their message of faith?

Ideas began popping up like the popcorn they were eating, and they made plans to invite other youth to join them in sharing their story. A team would be organized around music, testimonies, sharing the scriptures and prayer. They would tell their faith-story of God's action with them. Music from guitars, piano, voices and brass was woven into their plans.

Youthful enthusiasm bubbled over as they rehearsed and gave praise to the Lord. Yet, one ingredient was missing. What should they call themselves? How about "Ambassadors," or "Youtherans," or ?; the suggestions were many. Then it happened! Someone said, "I know a good name. Let's be 'Echoes.' We will only repeat what we have heard."

That's what it came to be. Twenty-three high school youth shared the gospel they had heard and studied. They did it in their home church, neighboring communities and a national youth event. They heard the gospel of Christ, and believing, they passed it on. Songs and stories of God's blessing from their own experiences could help others trust in Christ. They heard, "By grace we are saved through faith." They told it to others. Can you hear them? They have echoed those words of scripture, and others. Yes, God's Spirit used them.

Have you heard? Do you believe? Are you being an echo?

PRAYER:

Thank you, our Heavenly Father, for sending your son to be the savior of all. Help us confess our sins and need of forgiveness. Move us to believe in Jesus Christ, and then make us faithful "Echoes" of what we have heard about him. Help us echo your gospel. Amen.

FORGOTTEN? NEVER!

by Rev. Jack Jacobsen

"Can a woman forget her nursing child, or show no compassion for the child of her womb? Even these may forget, yet I will not forget you. See, I have inscribed you on the palms of my hands; your walls are continually before me." Isaiah 49:15-16.

Some of you retired pastors may be tempted at times to think that we have been forgotten. Forgotten by whom? Forgotten by the parishes where we served the people of God. Forgotten, too, by the members of those churches and even by our ministerial peers.

In the 49th chapter of the book of Isaiah, the prophet speaks of the restoration of Zion. He taught that God would restore Judah to Jerusalem from the exile in Babylon. Isaiah reminds them that their ultimate destiny was to be a light to the Gentiles and to bring salvation to the ends of the earth. This was not a new thought — God had made clear his intentions in the original covenant which had been given in Genesis 22:18. But Judah's desire for political greatness had obscured its original calling. Focused on its captivity in Babylon, Judah was not able to respond in joy when the prophet told them to rejoice now because God was going to use them again. The response of Judah was, *"The Lord has forsaken me, my Lord has forgotten me."* (Isaiah 49:14).

Forgotten? Zion's response was, "We are forsaken and forgotten." Then the Lord, speaking through the prophet, responded as quoted above from Isaiah 49.

Retirement may bring times when we feel that we are "on the shelf," placed aside as if we were no longer useful. No longer are we involved in the activities of the parish. We live in our memories and loneliness overtakes us. That loneliness turns into sorrow when we feel forgotten by the churches we have previously served. No longer are we remembered with the birthday cards, Christmas letters or casual letters. Those lonely feelings may tempt us to feel that even God has forgotten us.

But it is at this time that the Lord comes to us and whispers into our ears as he did to ancient Zion, "You are not forgotten by me." God told the church in Ephesus in Revelation 2, *I have not forgotten your hard work, your deeds and your perseverance."* So it is that the Lord reminds *us* that he remembers *our* years of work, ministry and perseverance in ministry to his redeemed saints.

Greater, perhaps, than being remembered by our Lord for years of service is the joy of knowing that the Lord has engraved our names on the palms of his hands. This took place at our baptism into his kingdom. With that engraving, we can never be forgotten by our Lord and Savior, Jesus Christ.

PRAYER:

Thank you, Lord, for the assurance that we are not forgotten by you. Our years of service to you and your kingdom on earth have been a source of joy and we shall someday celebrate with you in your kingdom in heaven. Amen.

THE LORD IS MY SHEPHERD

by Rev. J. Woodrow Jacobson

"The Lord is my shepherd, I shall not want. He makes me lie down in green pastures; he leads me beside still waters; he restores my soul. He leads me in right paths for his name's sake. Even though I walk through the darkest valley, I fear no evil; for you are with me; your rod and your staff — they comfort me. You prepare a table before me in the presence of my enemies; you anoint my head with oil; my cup overflows. Surely goodness and mercy shall follow me all the days of my life, and I shall dwell in the house of the Lord my whole life long." Psalm 23.

The 23rd Psalm of David is one of the wonders of the world. You like thousands of others can probably repeat it word for word. Its power to strengthen and comfort overwhelms one beyond understanding. In childhood its inclusion in evening devotions brings peaceful sleep with total resignation, and after a long life of many years this same power remains undiminished. No life crisis is too great for this magnificent Psalm to quiet our souls and cast out fears, for "the Lord is my shepherd, I shall not want."

Bill Landgraf, an operating room attendant at the Fairview Hospital some years ago (a beautiful Christian to all who knew him) suddenly found himself on the operating table one winter night with a life threatening blood clot in his leg, requiring emergency surgery. As the anesthetist began his work, Bill began repeating the 23rd Psalm, went to sleep midpoint, then when the surgeon had completed the delicate surgery, Bill awakened and completed the Psalm from the point where it had been interrupted an hour before. Through it all, the Good Shepherd had been very near. "Surely goodness and mercy shall follow me all the days of my life."

As her pastor, I was called to the home of an elderly woman
who had not responded to the voice of family for several days. In her weakness the end seemed near. I too received no response as the family gathered at her bedside. Then I began reading the 23rd Psalm, her favorite, and she opened her eyes, joined us in the familiar words of David and we prayed the Lord's Prayer together. She closed her eyes in peace and died a short time later. " . . . though I walk through the darkest valley, I fear no evil."

No less unforgettable was the reading of the Psalm to a young mother of teenaged twin daughters. The mother suffered from a painful, inoperable brain tumor. When one of the twins called me, she asked that I come quickly, her mother was hysterical and no one could calm her. My first words brought little change, but as I read the 23rd Psalm a quiet came over her. The hysteria was gone and she whispered, "The Lord *is* my shepherd ... I fear no evil, for thou art with me." We left the room and someone asked, "What did you do?" To which I replied, "It was not I who did it."

PRAYER:

Gracious God, we pray that your powerful word may go out through all the world, bringing its message of hope and help to all needy souls, even as it has come to us. Amen.

I REMEMBER CAROL

by Rev. Bernard W. Johnson

" . . . Be faithful until death and I will give you the crown of life." Revelation 2:10b.

I remember my first visit to the Miller home. There were three children under five. Two of them were twins. They were playing with the moving boxes. I was struck by their uninhibited happiness. Without success, their parents tried to quiet them, but they were having too much fun!

I reassured Bob and Carol that I was not perturbed by their shouts and laughter. It is always a pleasure to see happy children. Our meeting was pleasant and informal. This family had visited our church. Evidently they liked what they saw, because they kept coming back. Before long, they were members of this faith community.

They came to us with a living faith in Jesus as Savior. They had known before they met us that God was their Father, and that his promises were true. Before long they were key members in our congregation, faithfully attending services, volunteering for church chores, and spiritual sisters and brothers to the rest of us.

One scene at the back of my memory is of this family coming up for Holy Communion, with the children in tow for the pastor's blessing. Often, or should I say usually, these little ones were at their most cheery and unrestrained best as it came time for them to kneel. Shrewdly, they divided the children between parents. Child, parent, child, parent, child. When all was under control, about the time I got to them with the Host, Carol would roll her eyes heavenward as if to say, "I didn't think we would make it." Then she would smile and receive the Sacrament.

It was painful for me to say "goodbye" to this family when I retired. But not nearly as painful as returning to be with them a short time later because of Carol's sudden accidental death. Carol was a nurse. A good one. Returning home from work on a busy highway, Carol came upon a traffic accident. She did what the Good Samaritan did, stopping to offer her help. As she opened her door and put her feet on the pavement a car slammed into her and her car door. They said Carol died instantly.

At the funeral service I was invited to offer some pastoral comments. There in front of me was now a family of four instead of five. No need to hush them now. They were surrounded by a caring extended family, neighbors, and their congregational faith family. I don't even recall what I had to say. But surely my words were of love and of the Friend who never leaves us or abandons us.

Several years have passed, and we were back there recently. The Miller family has gotten on with their lives. On this particular visit Bob was serving as assisting minister. Now the roles were reversed; he was ministering to me. The children were there, one serving as an acolyte.

Carol was elsewhere. She was in the Father's House wearing that crown of life. Someday it will be so for each of us. Being faithful to death does not mean a perfect Christian, but a faithful one. Faithful means full of faith, faith in the savior, faith in God's promises. We do not have to hold our breath or cringe at the reality that our life may be shorter than we planned. It will all come out fine in the end. Our Friend has taken care of that.

PRAYER:

Thank you, O Father, for Jesus, and the knowledge that the sting of death has been removed for all who have their ultimate destiny at the resurrection of the body and the life everlasting. Amen.

A LITTLE CHILD IN MY LIFE

by Rev. Clarence Johnson

"God has great wisdom and understanding and by what Christ has done, God has shown us His own mysterious ways. Then when the time is right, God will do all that He has planned . . ." Ephesians 1:8-10.

On July 17, 1915, when I was three and one-half years old, my sister Clara was born. In the summer of 1918 she would play with us three older children for a little time and then got to sit on the steps of the house. First she would suck on her left thumb and at the same time pull on the lobe of her right ear. This followed by the singing, "Jesu Lille Lam Jeg Er" (Jesus Little Lamb I Am), followed by the praying of "Fader Vor" (Our Father). She repeated what I called a "ritual" several times during the day. Clara would play and pray.

When I was eight years old, I began seeing the formation of a cloud in the form of a small child lying on her back. At the age of twelve, I decided to spend my life telling people about Jesus. After that, I no longer saw the formation in the sky. This to me was my call into the ministry.

After a full ministry, I served sixteen years as Visitation Pastor in one church and four and a half years at a second church. Having resigned to have surgery, I am now fully mended. Thanks be to God! On January 18, 1997, I was 85 years old!

The following poem which I wrote in 1936 speaks of the importance of my sister Clara's life in my own life.

CLARA

She was a very precious soul
Filled with heaven's eternal light —
A radiant flower of God
Dispelling the blackness of night.

A little child with faith supreme,
Firmly grounded in Christ the Rock,
Meekly and humbly confessing
That she was a lamb of the flock.

Three years she journeyed among us,
Awaiting the call from glory.
Then, departing, left a message
Which has been beckoning me.

PRAYER:

Dear Heavenly Father, we thank you for special revelations in which you strengthen our faith and reinforce our calling to be your servants. In Jesus' name we pray, Amen.

REFRESH THE SAINTS

by Rev. Harvey M. Johnson

"I have indeed received much joy and encouragement from your love, because the hearts of the saints have been refreshed through you, my brother." Philemon 7.

Writing from prison, Paul, in this brief letter to his fellow worker Philemon, thanks him for his faith and love which "refreshed" the saints. He was asking him for a favor so that he might be refreshed as well.

There are some people in the church who refresh your spirit. I remember particularly one man in my first parish who was such a generous and gracious person. Though he had no more than a sixth grade formal education, he was self-educated in knowing how to make someone else feel good without using flattery. Quite often I would receive a note from him on Monday telling me how much he appreciated my Sunday sermon.

Although his own wife was suffering from cancer at the time, he greeted others with smiling good humor and would perform his plumbing services free of charge to those he felt could not afford to pay him. He was the first person to pledge significant amounts for building projects, missions, The Lutheran Bible Institute, and other causes. Though he lived modestly and had little wealth, he was rich in faith and love and enriched others by what he was.

How much do we refresh the saints? Perhaps there is a teacher or pastor or doctor, or some other person who has been a blessing to us. Do we ever say "thank you" or, in some other way, express our gratitude? There are so many things that can discourage us in our pilgrimage through life that can leave us feeling weary or discouraged. I believe that God wants us to refresh one another in Christ with a kind word or deed of encouragement along the way.

Let us resolve today to perform an act of kindness for a fellow worker and believer. We might be surprised to find that our own spirits have been refreshed as well.

PRAYER:

Dear God, we thank you that you have refreshed us with the gospel of Jesus Christ, and we thank you for fellow believers who have refreshed us when we needed it. Help us to refresh others, for Jesus' sake. Amen.

GOOD NEWS FOR
THE DISCOURAGED

by Rev. Manuel D. Johnson

"I, therefore, the prisoner in the Lord, beg you to lead a life worthy of the calling . . . for building up the body of Christ . . . as each part is working properly, promotes the body's growth in building itself up in love." Ephesians 4:1-16.

Imagine yourself becoming immobilized! A young woman received word that her disease and condition would not improve. She was crippled by a debilitating disease, and was told she would not walk again and would be confined to her bed for the remainder of her life.

She was a very positive, good spirited person and felt estranged from the community now that she could not actively participate in the everyday activities of the community of faith.

After discussing this and agreeing that we might pray and reflect on the situation, I came back for my weekly visit and asked if she would be interested in being on our prayer team. She could use the telephone, she had time to coordinate, and, most importantly, she believed in the power of prayer and had a great concern for people.

Serving on the prayer team became a great blessing to her. She became a great resource and blessing to others and now she felt as a partner in the ministry and was actively involved in the *"building up the body of Christ." Ephesians 4:12.*

God has given all people gifts that can be utilized in the kingdom work. The life journey of each of us is different and will affect how these gifts develop. It is for us to choose how we utilize these gifts. All people have a need to be a living part of the Body of Christ. The community of faith is called to provide opportunities for us to employ those gifts, grow in our faith and together celebrate God's presence, power and will. Jesus and the Apostle Paul write that it is the work of the Spirit that enables us to respond to that call.

"The fruit of the Spirit is love, joy, peace, patience, kindness, generosity, faithfulness, gentleness and self-control." Galatians 5:22. My friend possessed these gifts. The fleshly desires are opposed to the Spirit and prevent us from doing God's will.

The invitation, the Good News, is that God empowers us to be able to overpower the forces of the flesh, enables and wills for us to love and experience the joy of being God's people, building the Body of Christ and celebrating his presence.

PRAYER:

Dear God, grant us the joy of living. Help us to see and to use the gifts you have given us to the glory of your kingdom. Amen.

BUILDING THE FAITH
OF THE BUILDER

by Rev. Walter G. Johnson

"What is born of the flesh is flesh, and what is born of the Spirit is spirit. Do not be astonished that I said to you, 'You must be born from above.'" John 3:6-8

I had recently accepted a call to a church where there was a short two-person pew about three feet behind the left edge of the partially enclosed pulpit. With me on that pew sat one of the acolytes. There was no place to lay my hymnal and Bible. I had to be constantly putting them on the floor and picking them up again. A short bench would solve the problem.

Being new to the area I asked my secretary if she knew anybody who could make that little bench so it would match the wood and color of the rest of the chancel furniture. It was suggested that I contact the young man who had designed and built the baptismal font. But I was alerted to the fact that he was an atheist or at best an agnostic.

When he came over to look at the job we talked for a while about the church and faith in general. Then when we were on our knees behind the pulpit measuring for the right size for the bench I suggested that since we were already on our knees maybe we could pray about his faith in Jesus Christ. He said that he supposed it couldn't hurt and so we did.

I invited him to meet with me the following week and talk and pray some more. He accepted the invitation and we met for many, many weeks after that. One memorable evening he told me that he was ready to accept Jesus Christ as his Lord and Savior and was ready to be baptized.

What a glorious day it was for me to baptize Bob in the font that he had built earlier as an unbeliever!! What a joyous day for the members of the congregation, his wife and three little children!!

PRAYER:

Our Heavenly Father, I don't know who will be ready to hear your voice today. If it is somebody you place in my path may I be ready to witness to your love through our Savior, Jesus Christ. Amen.

A PLACE PREPARED!

by Rev. Raymond Klug

"And if I go and prepare a place for you, I will come again and will take you to myself, so that where I am, there you may be also."   John 14:3.

Jody was just fifteen years old when she was confirmed that spring. It was a rather large class for our average size congregation and because she was a quiet young lady there wasn't any reason to pay special attention to her. The fact that she was late for our confirmation picture brought her more notoriety than she was accustomed to.

It was that summer that she hurt her leg sliding into base while playing softball. In the fall when the pain persisted her parents took her to the doctor. The diagnosis was not good. A trip to the University Hospital determined that Jody had bone cancer and her leg would have to be amputated. Following the surgery we received the fateful news. The cancer had progressed too high into her pelvis and she had but a few weeks to live.

It was during one of my numerous visits with Jody that I asked her, "Jody, are you angry with God because you are dying?" I'm not sure why I asked the question, or what I expected her answer to be. But Jody simply said, "Oh no, Pastor, who could be angry with God?!"

Because Jody wanted to die at home she returned to the house in the country where she had grown. I sat by her bed and held her hand as we prayed. There wasn't a response anymore. Her parents offered me a cup of coffee as my wife took Jody's hand and softly sang "Jesus Loves Me." It was when the words "heaven's gate to open wide" filled the room that Jesus came and quietly took Jody to that place prepared for her.

Jesus has prepared a place for each one of us. He offered himself on the cross to pay the debt of our sin. May we have the faith of this young teenager and be as ready to meet him as Jody was.

PRAYER:

Heavenly Father, we know that we are always in your care. Strengthen our faith so that heaven's gate will be open wide for us at the end of our days. Amen.

USING BOTH HEAD AND HEART

by Rev. Harris W. Lee

"And this is my prayer, that your love may overflow more and more with knowledge and full insight to help you determine what is best . . ." Philippians 1:9-10a.

Christians are often seen as people with heart, people with compassion, empathy and heartfelt convictions.

This "heart" dimension is what often connects us with God. It involves us in prayer, worship and acts of mercy. Jesus apparently practiced this, withdrawing as he did for times of fasting and prayer to again be centered and grounded in God.

There is another dimension to the Christian life. People of heart, yes — but people of wisdom and discernment, too. People of knowledge and understanding. People of head as well as heart.

This is what Paul prays for in the text above. He prays not for more heart, but for more knowledge and insight. This is what will help us determine how to live faithful lives, he implies, knowledge and insight — the result of using your head. Jesus apparently practiced this, too, for the record gives evidence of planning his ministry, calculating the outcome of his actions, and of using imagination in his teaching.

It's not easy to keep the balance. Some follow the heart approach and are faithful in prayer and worship, but give little thought to the implications for daily life. Others follow the head approach and focus on understanding the faith and its appropriate expressions in daily life, yet lack motivation for actually living it out. What is needed is a balance of head and heart.

The heart dimension helps you keep your thoughts and feelings in tune with the call of God to trust and follow. When you pray your thinking is influenced. You become mentally receptive to the will of God. But how do you know the will of God in your particular situation? It is usually the result of study, reflection, discernment — yes, and in the congregation, even debate and participative decision-making.

The balance of head and heart is therefore important not only in one's personal life; it is important as well when exercising leadership in the life of the congregation. When planning the congregation's life and mission, for example, prayer and worship attune the people to God and remind them that God calls them to be his servants, gives them purpose and promise — all of which is activity of the heart. But it is the head that discerns the times, and the setting for the congregation's mission, determining available resources, setting realistic goals, charting a course of action.

Perhaps the key is to honor Christ's call to love and serve God with heart, soul, mind and strength — in short, with both head and heart.

PRAYER:

Lord God, may this be our resolve this day, that our "love may overflow more and more with knowledge and full insight" and thereby be faithful to your call. Amen.

A DESERT EXPERIENCE

by Rev. Laurel V. ("Bud") Lindberg

The apostle Paul wrote, *"be filled with the Spirit . . . giving thanks to God the Father at all times and for everything in the name of our Lord Jesus Christ."* *Ephesians 5:18, 20.*

A humorous story is told about two men who were walking through a field in which they spotted an enraged bull. Understandably, they darted toward the nearest fence with the storming critter in hot pursuit. When it became apparent they wouldn't make it, one shouted to the other, "Put up a prayer, John!" John answered, "I can't. I've never prayed a public prayer in my life!" "But you gotta," his companion implored, "he's gaining on us!" "O.K.," panted John, "but the only prayer I know is one my Dad used to say at the table: 'O Lord, for what we are about to receive, make us truly thankful.'"

Of course, we should give thanks always, but we all know there are times when that's easier to do than others. No one would, in his right mind, intentionally cross a bull-occupied field, nor would one choose a desert. But deserts aren't all bad! For there are things to be discovered there which one could never discover elsewhere. One thing: there aren't many places to hide! For a wilderness often exposes our humanness, our vulnerability, our dependence. But amidst it all, one discovers that our dear Lord is there, too...and life...and love.

Such was our family's discovery while crossing one of those arid places several years ago during brain surgery on our youngest daughter, Maren, the mother of two infant sons. There was much darkness. But there was also the light! Early surgery became possible through the kind intervention of a dear friend, an orthopedic surgeon at Scottsdale's Mayo who arranged an appointment at Rochester's Mayo. Furthermore, the tumor was operable and benign. There were also the love and countless prayers of dear friends near and far. Never had we felt greater power and love. And I have a hunch that the surgeons felt it too, since the surgery went flawlessly. Afterward, one of them confided that they had "never seen anything quite like it. We call it 'a miracle'." In a desert, we had discovered anew God's goodness and mercy, certainly not by our merit, but simply by his amazing grace.

Life and love are truly gifts from God. We can't buy, earn or deserve them. They are gifts! Not to be kept, but to be shared. As St. Francis so beautifully phrased it, "Lord, make me an instrument of thy peace ... for it is in giving (passing on the gift to others) ... that we receive" (more to share). So may it be with us.

PRAYER:

Dear Heavenly Father, thanks for your abiding Presence, even in our deserts. Fill us with your Spirit so we may flow out to others, through Jesus Christ, our Lord. Amen.

A QUICK ANSWER TO PRAYER

by Rev. Herbert G. Loddigs

"Before they call I will answer; while they are yet speaking I will hear." Isaiah 65:24

In World War II the Japanese had beaten me during interrogation. They beat my friend to death. After they imprisoned me I felt forsaken. I cried out to God, "I need a New Testament. The Japanese took mine. I must have one. Oh God, get me a New Testament." I thought, "How can God get a New Testament to me in a jail cell in the Philippines where New Testaments were almost unknown?"

When I was through praying, a woman in another cell called out, "Are you a Christian?"

I answered, "Yes."

She then asked, "Do you have a New Testament?"

"I don't even have one for myself. I have none for you."

She then said, "I have two. Here is one."

She threw it from her cell into mine. It landed at my feet. What a quick answer to prayer!

I thanked her and asked, "Why did you have two New Testaments?"

She said, "A Japanese officer asked me to go dancing with him. I knew he wanted more than dancing. I refused. He got angry and said, 'You have insulted the Imperial Japanese Army. I'm taking you to prison!'"

"I took two New Testaments so I would have one to give away."

Later, she was released.

God was answering my prayer before I even prayed it. She was his messenger. I am sure she was grateful God could use her in this way.

During the rest of the eleven weeks I was in the jail, I was able to read from that New Testament to my fellow jail-mates including young men from the Salvation Army as well as many criminals. I gave them a course in the New Testament, including Luther's explanation of the Third Article of the Creed. Even the criminals were very kind to me.

I sensed the power of many who were praying for me — men, women and children. Three years later, after I was rescued, I found this was true. They had been praying for me every day.

Because this woman suffered pain and indignities, this gave me the opportunity to bear witness to the Gospel for the prisoners, a witness they would not have otherwise heard.

PRAYER:

Thank you, Lord. It is by your decision, not by our own, that we have been saved and kept. Amen.

PRAYING UP A STORM

by Rev. Philip R. Luttio

"Bless the Lord . . . who forgives all your iniquity . . . who redeems your life from the Pit." Psalm 103:1-5.

I'm a young teenager, and I'm invited to a Bible camp! It ought to be a blast! Yes, with sports, new friends and all. Then one night it happened. I had prepared ahead of time by sitting in the very last row so I could be first out when the evening meeting was over.

But it didn't get over. Instead, it began "eternity" — or my relationship to it!

Actually, I was brought up in a Christian home and had agreed with everything taught, including the fact that everyone was a sinner. And of course, I was one — but no worse than anyone else . . . or so I thought. That is, until that kindly-voiced speaker started way up there at the far end of the dining hall-turned-meeting room.

I thought that I was almost invisible back there on the last bench. But that preacher all but named my name as he described how my so-called "little sins" had actually nailed Jesus to the tree . . . and how I myself was the guilty one! That *Cross* should be *my* punishment!

I wanted to run straight out the door. I couldn't. I was trapped in death row. I had never felt so horrible in all my life.

O how thankful I am that Dr. O. C. Hanson did not stop preaching at that point. He closed the message with the most glorious news ever heard. He said,

"You don't have to take that punishment. Jesus actually took it in your place. So now you are absolutely free!"

Can you imagine? My heart was pounding. I'd gone from the deepest misery into the electrifying heights of ecstasy.

As soon as possible I got back to the cabin, pulled out a postcard and wrote to my mom saying, "All that you ever prayed for me has happened. Now I know what you've always wanted for me."

My mom had indeed "prayed up a storm," arranging behind the scenes to get her son up to camp under the powerful ministry of Dr. Oscar C. Hanson. And she understood precisely what that postcard meant.

After World War II, I got back to study at The Lutheran Bible Institute under Dr. Hanson. Several years later Margaret and I were privileged to have him preach both at our wedding and at our commissioning service — going to bring that good news to the people of Japan. We had 38 years of opportunity to share that tremendous word of release in that country!

We thank the Lord for using LBI and Dr. Hanson to get the waves of the gospel moving from the shores of a little Bible camp in the Midwest to splash across the Pacific to those dry and needy folk there.

PRAYER:

Lord, help me to see how your tremendous work of love on that tree was indeed done for me. And therefore you transform my life to be able to share Your gift of love with others, right here, even today. Amen.

WHEN LOVE REPLACES HATE

by Rev. Herman F. Mansur

"For I am not ashamed of the gospel: it is the power of God for salvation to everyone who has faith, to the Jew first and also to the Greek." Romans 1:16.

During our first year as missionaries to a newly opened primitive area of the highlands of New Guinea, we soon became aware of much tension and rivalry among the various tribes, which often resulted in open hostility and warfare. Subsequently, they were rounded up by the local police, and herded to the nearest stockade or "kalabus," where they were forced to live and work together for many months. After the incarceration, they would return to their respective villages, only to repeat the cycle of animosity, hatred, and fear of one another.

Seven years later, as some people of these various tribes had come to hear the "Miti" (good news), some had requested further instruction in catechism and worship in preparation for baptism. Obviously, this first baptism would be a totally new experience for them. Therefore, as part of the preparation, they decided to leave their respective villages and build a single village for all near the future site of the baptism. When asked about this daring move, an elderly man of wisdom rose to his feet and said: "We have been living as enemies for generations. We were consumed with suspicions, hatred, and killing that kept us apart. We knew only about revenge and 'pay-backs.' Now the Miti (gospel) has come and taught us about Jesus and his love; about reconciliation through forgiveness; and how we are all brothers and sisters in Christ through baptism. So we have come to prove to ourselves that we can truly live together in peace and love as brothers and sisters. If not, then we are *not* ready yet to call ourselves Christians."

After living together in peace and harmony for more than a year, all 168 of them decided to be baptized. The day before the baptism, when all items of black-magic, sorcery, warfare (spears, bows and arrows) were publicly burned, the elder mounted the platform and once again professed: "The police, guns, and kalabus could force us to act like brothers for awhile, but it is the Gospel that changed our hatred into love and our revenge into forgiveness. Now we have become reconciled and we can live as one single tribe or family."

Having personally witnessed the power of the Gospel, Romans 1:16 became, and still is, one of my favorite scripture verses.

PRAYER:

O Lord, all around us in this world there is hatred, hostility, warfare, and revenge. May your kingdom come, O Lord, through the teaching, preaching, and demonstration of your Gospel by each one of us. Amen.

SUSTAINED BY THE SPIRIT

by Rev. B. F. Meschke

" . . . even to your old age I am he, even when you turn gray I will carry you. I have made, and I will bear; I will carry and will save." Isaiah 46:4.

People tell us that as we advance to old age the short-term memory begins to weaken. Things that happened fifty or sixty years ago are well remembered, but things that happened last month, or yesterday, are gone.

Is it possible that the long-term memory has slipped a bit, too? Sometimes we talk about the "good old days," but would we really want them back? Oh, we become rather proud and a bit boastful when we talk with our grandchildren about the hard times we had to live through. When the teenage grandchild complains about having a job that pays only five dollars an hour, we boast a little about how we used to work for a dollar a day. We tell about our mother who had to add water to the soup so everyone in the family could have some. Television? We didn't even have a radio! We had to walk to school, too, and later we worked our way through college by waiting on tables and working in a grocery store on Saturdays. Nobody ever told us that we were poor; we didn't know it.

Oh, come now! It wasn't all that bad, was it? If it was, why do we so much enjoy talking about it now? Well, maybe our long-term memory has slipped a bit and we do not recall the things that weren't so good in years past. It is just as well. There are better things to talk about.

To all of us — to Israel in Isaiah's time, to us today, to our children and to all who follow — our Lord says, "I am he who will sustain you." He has done so in the past. He will do so always for his people. "He who did not spare his own Son, but gave him up for us all — how will he not also, along with him, graciously give us all things?" (Romans 8:32).

Through the years the message of God's love in Christ has come to us through the Scriptures, and through us that message has gone out to many others. In his mercy toward us, God did not spare his own Son. He gave him to suffering and death, bearing the penalty and punishment for our sin. Because of Christ's work we are forgiven. Through faith in Christ we are at peace with God. Covered with Christ's righteousness we stand before God holy and pure in his sight. We trust in Christ for our eternal welfare and salvation. The Holy Spirit sustains us in that faith. Rich or poor in things of the body, we are immensely and eternally rich in God's sustaining love in Christ.

In a few years our children will probably be talking to their grandchildren about their "good old days." May they echo the message that we live, body and soul, through the sustaining love of God shown us in Jesus Christ, our Savior.

PRAYER:

Father in heaven, sustain us in faith in Christ Jesus that by your grace we may share in the glory he has won and prepared for us. Amen.

ALONE, YET NOT ALONE

by Rev. Gerhard C. Michael, Sr.

"For in him we live and move and have our being. . ."
Acts 17: 28.

Once we have experienced the blessing of God upon
what would be called a successful ministry of more
than half a century, Satan tempts us to lose sight of
how dependent we are upon our Heavenly Father.
We are in need of listening to Paul say to the
Athenians and us, "For in him we live, and move, and
have our being." This was driven home to me during
1996. I have been living alone on the edge of Howard
Lake since my spouse of more than 57 years died in
1990. Unbeknownst to me, I had suffered a so-called
"silent heart attack."

Some might call it a coincidence that my pastor son in
Georgia called to inquire about my wellbeing. Being
disturbed at my response, he called his sister, a nurse,
who in turn called me the next day to get a promise
from me to see the doctor. The result was a stay in
the Buffalo Hospital with moderate heart damage
with subsequent good recovery without surgery.
This was all due to God's loving care, emphasizing
for me how dependent I was and am on his loving
care, showing me that although I appeared to be
alone, I really was *not* alone.

I was reminded of this again, even more
emphatically, last December in the middle of the
afternoon when I fell on the ice on my driveway and
broke my hip. Since this was in an out of the way
place, my cry "help!!" brought no response.
Fortunately, the temperature was just above freezing
and I was able to drag myself about forty feet to the
shelter of the garage. When lights came on at the

neighbor's house several hours later, my cry for "help" reached his ear and caused him to come to help me. When I reached the hospital my body temperature was at 91 degrees.

Lying on the cold concrete, I had time to reflect on how dependent I was on my Lord and Savior, who had given his Son into death for my salvation. I could call on him for help, for I knew that he loved me. Although I was alone and helpless, I knew that I was not alone. I could recall his wonderful promises of help in his word. It has made me all the more thankful to him for showing me his love through my children, who helped me under his blessing to recover well. Truly it is in him that "we live, and move, and have our being."

PRAYER:

Thank you, Lord, for your love in reminding us how totally dependent we are upon your loving care. In Jesus' name. Amen.

MEMORIAL

by Erna C. (Miller) Shenk
In honor of my father, The Rev. Frank Miller,
who in 1996 went home to be with the Lord.

"This people honors me with their lips, but their hearts are far from me; in vain do they worship me, teaching human precepts as doctrines." Matthew 15:8-9.

As a graduate of Hamma Divinity School in Ohio under the headship of Dean Flack, Dad was fiercely in support of basic Lutheran fundamentals of doctrine. Taking time away from pastoring, Dad lent his talents to be editor of *Lutherans Alert Magazine,* a publication that informed Lutherans about what was going on in their own denomination. He was seeing anti-Biblical teachings emanate from Lutheran pulpits. The idea that the Bible in the original texts was not wholly inspired by God was abhorrent to him. Some "pastors" would even preach that Christ was not virgin-born nor truly resurrected. His heart for Bible camp was broken seeing young people taught that it was more important to "know yourselves" than to know God.

Dad is with his Lord and Savior now. His prayers were that his fellow Lutherans would turn back to Scripture and basic fundamental Lutheran doctrine. He preached the word for over thirty years and the importance of acknowledging Christ as Savior.

"Then he called the crowd to him and said to them, 'Listen and understand: it is not what goes into the mouth that defiles a person, but it is what comes out of the mouth that defiles.'" (Matthew 15:10-11)

PRAYER:

Lord, help us to know your truth. Amen.

GOD'S PLAN FOR US

by Rev. Dr. Orval K. Moren

"For surely I know the plans I have for you, says the Lord, plans for your welfare and not for harm, to give you a future with hope." Jeremiah 29:11.

A deputation team from The Lutheran Bible Institute had been invited to present a youth program in the Gethsemane Lutheran Church in Upsala, Minnesota. I had been asked to drive my old but reliable car. I was reluctant because, I thought, they need my car — not me. Several students came to assure me that I was invited and my car was secondary. In fact, if I didn't want to drive that was just fine. Finally, I was convinced. I would participate.

It was a cold Saturday in February. We arrived early in the afternoon. There were lots of kids at that church eager to meet us and enjoy our time together.

As I entered the church, there was a stairway just off to the left. I stepped onto the landing of the first step and looked down the stairway. Looking up to see who was coming was a young woman who was one of the youth leaders. I looked directly at her. She looked back at me. I took a second, then a third look. Wow! Now who was this?

I was single and free of any special person in my life. I was searching and praying about my life partner. Who was *this* person?

I asked Vivian Westman, one of the LBI leaders. Laughingly, she said, "She is my sister. Do you want to meet her?" I replied, "Of course I want to meet her."

That evening, and the next day, I spent as much time with my newly found friend as possible. When the time for us to depart was at hand, I asked if I could write. "Yes," she said. I did! Our life together began.

The Lutheran Bible Institute was the medium through which the Lord brought his blessing to Bernell Westman and me. To us have been born four lovely children. They, in turn, have continued to bless us with nine grandchildren.

PRAYER:

Lord Jesus, you have used many different people to bless our lives. I thank you for my life with Bernell, and the blessings I have received through the many students of The Lutheran Bible Institute. Thank you, Lord. Amen.

SUPPLYING OUR NEEDS

by Rev. Dr. Orval K. Moren

"And my God will fully satisfy every need of yours according to his riches in glory in Christ Jesus."
Philippians 4:19.

I had been planning to visit my girlfriend, Bernell Westman, who later became my wife. Bernell lived about 100 miles away and I desperately wanted to visit her again. My car was old, yet reliable. But I had no spare money!

I had prayed about my opportunity to visit with her at her home. Often, when I was out of money, she would help me return to LBI from Upsala by paying for a tank of gas. I knew of her care and generosity so I planned accordingly.

Before I left on Friday afternoon for my three-hour drive, I checked my mail box. Inside was a small envelope with my name on it: Orval Moren. I usually signed my name to include the initial "K". This person knew me, but not all that well, I thought to myself.

I opened the envelope. In it was a check for $15! It was written out to me but there was no other identification except the signature on the check. It was a name I didn't recognize. Who was this person who would favor me? I didn't have a clue. Even to this day, I don't have any knowledge of the donor.

I believed the promise recorded by the Apostle Paul to the Philippians. "The Lord will supply your needs." I have thought about his verse many times. The word says, "needs", not "wants." There is a difference.

In thanking the Lord for my experience at The Lutheran Bible Institute, which so powerfully shaped my life, I have also thanked him for the generosity of this unknown person. It was a little gift with unforgettable results!

PRAYER:

Lord Jesus, I thank you for the influence of LBI in my life, and how you have used people to bless other people. Such blessing is sacramental, like the community of faith, the Body of Christ. Thank you, Lord. Amen.

LIVING BY THE BOOK

by Rev. Maynard L. Nelson

"But strive first for the Kingdom of God and his righteousness . . ." Matthew 6:33.

Which book do you live by? The date book — or the word of God? Christians are supposed to live by the "Good Book," but sometimes we let the cares of life overwhelm us and control our lives. Often it can be for worthy causes — but even the good can crowd out the best. We Americans are activists and we can become so busy that we have no time to talk with God or hear his word.

Pastors can even be guilty of this. For years Augsburg Fortress has sent Lutheran pastors a little red appointment book that we carry with us. It usually becomes quickly filled with appointments for meetings, weddings, funerals, baptisms, and counseling sessions. If we are not careful, it becomes a hard taskmaster, and the date book controls our lives instead of using it to be in control of life. It is even possible to have little time left to spend with God or our family.

Some years ago I was forced to face this issue when I lost my "little red book." Actually, I left my appointment book in my shirt pocket and it went through the wash. All that I could recover was the ragged red cover. All my dates and busy schedule went down the drain. At first I panicked, but then I thought, "What difference will it make ten years from now or even from the point of view of eternity?"

In the Sermon on the Mount, Jesus asks his followers, "Why do you worry about clothes and food and drink?" He tells them that his Father knows their need and they should rather put his kingdom and righteousness first. If we do that today, then tomorrow will take care of itself. He wasn't telling us not to plan for tomorrow, but rather to trust our Heavenly Father for both today and tomorrow. You can be sure that there will be sufficient cares and problems for tomorrow, but you can also be certain that his grace will be sufficient, no matter what may come! If we live by the Book of Books, we will be abundantly blessed by the promises of God!

PRAYER:

Lord, too often our lives are out of control and our hearts are filled with anxiety. Forgive us for not putting first things first and help us to live by the promises of your word today and to trust you fully for tomorrow. For Jesus' sake, Amen.

A PASSPORT TO THE KINGDOM

by Rev. Maynard L. Nelson

"Jesus answered, "Very truly, I tell you, no one can enter the Kingdom of God without being born of water and Spirit." John 3:5.

It was time to board the plane for the flight home to America after an exciting mission tour in LaPaz, Bolivia. In a moment of distraction, a thief grabbed our purse with our passports, and my wife and I found ourselves in a foreign land without documentation. It's a strange and scary feeling not to belong and to be denied passage by immigration authorities.

We were greatly relieved when we finally had our passports restored by the U.S. Embassy in LaPaz. Later, when we returned to the United States, I was never so proud as to present my U.S. passport and be admitted to this great country as a citizen.

Nicodemus was seeking when he came to Jesus at night and asked him how to gain entrance to the Kingdom of God. We read in John 3:5 that Jesus answered, "I tell you the truth; no one can enter the Kingdom of God unless he is born of water and the Spirit."

I happened to be born into citizenship in the United States of America. I didn't buy it, I didn't earn it, I didn't even deserve it. Yet, it is one of the most precious gifts that I possess and it's really all by grace. There are others, though, who have paid the price for my freedoms and privileges as an American citizen.

It is also true that I have not earned my place in the Kingdom of God. Jesus Christ paid the price on

Calvary's cross that I might enter the kingdom and belong to God's family and enjoy the freedoms and privileges as a child of God. We, too, are born into this relationship through the waters of baptism and the work of the Holy Spirit. That's how the grace of our Lord Jesus Christ comes to us.

If you have any question about your membership in God's kingdom or your place in heaven, then look at the document of his word. There you will find the promises of our Savior and the assurances that you have a passport to eternal salvation by the grace of God. Receive it, enjoy it — and be thankful!

PRAYER:

Gracious God, thank you for the free gift of salvation and the privilege of membership in your eternal kingdom, through Jesus Christ, our Lord. Amen.

IT IS O.K. TO TRY
BUT BETTER TO PRAY!

by Rev. Robert S. Nelson

"Even though I walk through the darkest valley, I fear no evil; for you are with me; . . ." Psalm 23:4.

This year (1997) I will be celebrating the 50th Anniversary of my ordination. I have stories to tell, but there is a very personal one that helped set my course for prayer.

 Our first son, John Mark, was born in Caribou, Maine, and was very small. The two rural congregations that I served had invited Dr. Granlund of LBI to preach at the services the next day. His train had been delayed. With his usual charm and wit he said, "I was late that someone more important might arrive first!"

John's immune system was not fully operative and he developed a fungus infection of the mouth. Our doctor realized that John's only chance to live was to fly him to a children's hospital 300 miles away. The doctors there examined him and told us, "He has fungus pneumonia, and we don't know if we can save him."

What a blow! We cried in terror and fear. We forgot the
promises made by God in John's baptism. So this was the end of it all? I learned a lesson I would never forget that would be full of God's promises for a ministry of telling others about *ONE* who cared for everyone and listened to their cries. There was a knock on the door, and the woman who made the beds saw our reddened eyes and asked what was wrong with us.   So we told her about our beloved

little baby. She said, "Have you tried prayer?"
Ashamed, we looked at each other. I didn't thank her
or even ask her name. But we did pray as we held
hands.

We flew home with the promise to call the hospital
every day. Two weeks and hundreds of prayers later
we returned to the hospital. There Dr. Goldberg, a
dedicated Jewish doctor, met us and handed little
John Mark to his smiling and gently crying mother.
As we were about to thank him he held up his hand
and said, "Someone else did this!" What a lesson to
share!

PRAYER:

*Thank you, God. Not only for John's healing, but for this
lesson in ministry. Amen.*

PRAISE THE LORD!

by Rev. J. A. Nestingen

"Praise the Lord! Praise the Lord, O my soul! I will praise the Lord as long as I live; I will sing praise to my God all my life long."   Psalm 146:1-2.

The Psalmist often breaks into songs of thanksgiving and praise. He praises and thanks God for all his wonderful work, and for his loving kindness down through the generations. If we page through our hymnals, we find many hymns that echo the Psalmist's words. I am certain that you, too, find yourself reflecting on such Psalms and hymns. Yes, I'm certain that in your own personal life you have broken out in song and praise, just as the Psalmist.

Thanksgiving and praise are in the heart and soul of every child of God. If we count our blessings from day to day, we will find much to be thankful for. Years ago I read that Stonewall Jackson said he never took a drink of water without thanking God for the "water of life."

My mind often goes back to a little old homestead shack in western North Dakota where I served my first parish. I remember it well and the lesson taught me by a weather-beaten old Norwegian immigrant lady who was picking flowers from her prolific flower bed as we visited.

Plucking a beautiful blossom, she held it high for me to see and said, "We tink we're so blame shmart, but only God can make a flower!" God the creator was uppermost in her mind. She declared her praises in a simple but powerful way.

We, too, are thankful for the beauty of the earth and join our praises with Christians everywhere. God is in our hearts, souls and minds at all times. He is the Creator of all things and we are the benefactors, the recipients of his goodness. Not only this, but out of his love he has sent our Savior, Jesus Christ the Redeemer. He is the Rock of our salvation. It is for this we sing our song of unending praise and thanksgiving. "Praise the Lord, O my Soul!"

PRAYER:

O Lord, may I always have a thankful heart and sing your praises. Amen.

THE SECRET OF THE SNOW

by Rev. Harold L. Olson

"Have you entered the storehouses of the snow . . ."
Job 38:22a.

After taking many pictures of beautiful snow, I
became intrigued by the fact that it can serve so well
as a breathing blanket for grass, plants and small
bushes. It can also be compacted to form snowballs,
snowmen, ski trails and even hard roads for cars and
heavy trucks, and can disappear with a bright sun to
become water for all living things.

When reading Job, I was further intrigued as to why
God asked him, "Have you stood on the threshold of
the snow?" Or in another translation, "Have you
considered the treasuries of the snow?" Job's sore
affliction, though so much greater than mine, had
attracted my attention since I had a rash of boils on
my back while playing basketball in high school. The
doctor lanced them until he found a better remedy.
Job's pain was multiplied when the group therapy
which his friends applied made him more frustrated
than ever. Even his plea of integrity could not offset
this.

Why did God ask him these questions? One day I
decided to stand at the threshold and what did I see?
Although so very different, each snowflake had the
God-given ability to meld with others to form a
protective cover; to mesh with each other to make
something compact, firm and solid. Last of all, to
melt together to be drops of water to satisfy the thirst
of all living things.

Was Job melding? Meshing? Melting? Yes. Melding
took place when he listened to God and came back for

more; meshing when he asked for forgiveness; melting when he prayed to God for his friends, "and the Lord accepted Job's prayer."

PRAYER:

Lord Jesus, you as a babe in Bethlehem melded with all humanity. As the Messiah, you meshed with all who longed and looked for you. And as the Lamb of God you melted, laying down your life for your sheep and your friends. Grant to us, by your Holy Spirit, that same gift, so that our lives may be to your glory, for the good of others, and to our own soul's satisfaction. Amen.

A CALL TO PRAYER

by Captain Bernt C. Opsal
CHC, USNR-RET

"In the same way, let your light shine before others, so that they may see your good works and give glory to your Father in heaven." Matthew 5:16.

During times of threatening war or national crisis it is not so difficult to remember our men and women serving on *our* behalf in the armed forces. But in periods of so-called "peace times" we tend to forget about them. And yet they need our concern and prayers.

Having had the privilege to serve in the U.S. Navy as a chaplain in World War II, during the Korean Conflict and in the reserves for over twenty-nine years, I know from personal experience what a *difference* it makes to have the church and members of the local congregation backing you up. It is tough to live as a Christian anywhere, but believe me — it can be very difficult when you are in the military. The *milieu* in which a service person lives often is not conducive to upholding Christian standards, to say the least. The *pressures* on a person living away from home and upon family and loved ones can, at times, be very, very difficult.

How *they* need our prayers; as do the chaplains who minister to them; their officers, who lead them; as well as their families, who support them and all too often are separated from them. What a difference it makes when the individual has a vital faith with a living relationship to our Lord and Savior, Jesus Christ, in whom a baptismal covenant has been established!

I recall while aboard ship one of the crew, a machinist, came to see me. He stated that Dan, who was in his company, was always willing to be of help in any way he could. We were overseas at the time and he was always willing to stand by on duty when another guy wanted to get off the ship. He did this, in spite of the fact that others would make fun of him because he read his Bible in his bunk, always attended church services, often went to Bible study, led an exemplary life, and was always helpful and cooperative. He stood the ribbing from the guys with a smile, even when it went almost to the point of ridicule. But what was even worse for them was that he was the best machinist in the shop. His work was masterful!

"Chaplain, what does he have that I don't have?" Jim asked. "He has the Lord Jesus Christ," the chaplain answered. "Then I want him too," the seeking sailor said. And so the chaplain led him into the scriptures and showed him the way of salvation. By the grace of God, he came to the assurance of his faith and peace with his living savior. Now Jim became active in the religious activities aboard ship and later became a leader of the spiritually minded lay people aboard when Dan was transferred in the Seventh Fleet in the Pacific area.

PRAYER:

Dear Heavenly Father, we thank you for all the pastors and lay people in our congregations who remember our men and women in the armed forces of our country. We pray for those in the service who conscientiously witness for their Lord by attitude, word and deed. Give wisdom to our military leaders, especially the President of the United States. May they also provide moral leadership as well. In the name of Jesus Christ our Lord and Savior. Amen.

TRUST AND LISTEN TO THE LORD

by Rev. Dr. Russell E. Osnes

"God is our refuge and strength, a very present help in trouble." Psalm 46:1.

Our youngest son was diagnosed as a brittle diabetic when he was 2 1/2 years old. Brittle means he was subject to insulin reactions and/or a coma with little or no warning. An active and energetic little boy, he required constant supervision. He was not old enough to understand what was going on.

One Sunday morning he was in the nursery while I was conducting the morning service. His mother was at the organ. During the sermon a nursery assistant came in to get my wife and moments later came in for our family doctor. I watched all of this while I continued to preach. I knew something was happening to our son and was greatly concerned about him. Being a young, goal-directed pastor I did not want to interrupt my sermon and I trusted the Lord, my wife, and the doctor.

Later, I learned Jeffrey had suddenly lapsed into an insulin reaction. They did mouth-to-mouth resuscitation in order to keep him alive, while the doctor retrieved his bag from his car to administer intravenous glucose which saved his life. The doctor told us he had thought of Jeffrey a few days before and had put a syringe filled with glucose in his bag, for just such an emergency.

That old hymn, "In the Garden", sings of the Lord walking and talking with us. That is what life is about, to walk and talk with the Lord. As we listen and talk we are led by the Spirit. The doctor, a new Christian, listened and acted. We, as parents, learned to listen and act, and to trust. He experienced other "close calls" over the last 30 years but we, he himself, or others were prepared to help. He lives a near normal life, is on an insulin pump, is married, works full time, listens to his body, his Lord — and acts, trusting God.

The psalmist is right. God is our refuge and strength. God will help us and others prepare for trouble if we will listen as did our doctor.

PRAYER:

Thank you, Lord Jesus, for the fellowship we have with you; that we can find refuge in you and that you walk and talk with us to bring direction, peace, and joy to our lives. We will listen. Amen.

GOD'S SPIRIT WORKS

by Rev. Paul Pallmeyer

"And these are the ones sown on the good soil: they hear the word and accept it and bear fruit, thirty and sixty and a hundredfold." Mark 4:20.

Sometimes the work of sharing the Good News of Jesus can be frustrating, sometimes thrilling. As a missionary in Japan in the early 1950's, I experienced both.

Here's one of the happier stories: I had only been in Japan about a year and a half when a young man began attending our weekly Bible class and church service. Several months later he asked if he could be baptized and a short time later joined our small fellowship of Christians in Fukagawa on the island of Hokkaido in northern Japan. At Christmas the group celebrated with a party at which we sang songs, ate goodies, and told stories. Those who had been baptized during the previous twelve months were expected to share how they had come to faith.

"When I first started attending the Bible Class," said the young man who had recently been baptized, "I was a Communist. I came to spy on you people. I wanted to make fun of you. I heard your preacher, who could hardly speak Japanese, telling you about Jesus, and I wondered how you could believe such nonsense."

"Because I was fascinated, I kept coming and began to hear in a different way. Could this really be true? After a while, I realized that I was beginning to believe the message of Jesus, too, and I left Communism and asked to be baptized."

So God's Spirit works. Persons who seem least likely to come to faith do so as they hear God's word even when the language is poor or stated in a clumsy way. Jesus told Nicodemus, *"The wind blows where it chooses, and you hear the sound of it; but you do not know where it comes from or where it goes. So it is with everyone who is born of the Spirit."* John 3:8.

PRAYER:

Spirit of God, speak to us and renew our faith through your holy word. Remove from us a hesitancy to share that word because of a lack of language skills or fear that the one hearing the message will not accept it. Amen.

A LESSON FROM THE CORN

by Rev. Daniel W. Pearson

"For we know that if the earthly tent we live in is destroyed, we have a building from God, a house not made with hands, eternal in the heavens." *2 Corinthians 5:1.*

Emma was her name. When I came to Wadena as a newly ordained pastor she was 87 years old. We got to know one another after church during the summer months. She lived on the farm. Her son John lived with her and took care that the farm was productive.

Fall came and harvest time. After church that beautiful October Sunday, Emma shook hands with me and invited me to coffee the next Monday afternoon.

She had the table set when I came into the driveway and walked up to the house. The steps to the large porch faced a large cornfield. John was cutting down some corn to feed the cattle.

Emma looked at me and smiled. I wanted you to sit here with me, because you are young and you don't know very much yet, even if you have been to college and seminary.

She pointed toward the corn field. "See, John cuts the corn. I watch each stalk. Each one reminds me of a loved one, a friend, a neighbor. You will find as the years fly by that there will come a time when you realize that you have more loved ones on the other side than you have on this side. Then you know that God has given you a long life and you always give thanks for the host of friends who will greet you when your earthly tent is taken down and you move into that permanent house that is prepared for his own."

Emma looked at me across her coffee cup and said, "I have reached the day. For me, it's harvest time. I pray God blesses you, too."

We sat quietly for some minutes. The day moves toward me with every harvest.

PRAYER:

Lord, keep each of us in fellowship with your saints in Jesus until we are all together again. Amen.

JESUS AND MY OWN AGING

by Rev. Dr. Robert N. Pearson

Jesus never grew old. How then could he know our problems? What problems? Listen to the writer of Ecclesiastes:

"In the day when the guards of the house tremble, and the strong men are bent, and the women who grind cease working because they are few, and those that look through the windows see dimly . . . and the mourners will go about the streets; before the silver cord is snapped, and the golden bowl is broken . . ." Ecclesiastes 12:3-6.

Yes, aging has a way of making the strong bent; our eyesight grows dim, our hearing fails, our friends get sick and die. We get lonely. We wonder about the future. The only references I find where Jesus speaks about aging are to his mother when he was on the cross.   And to Peter after the resurrection. To his mother, Jesus asked her to consider John as one who would look after her. (John 19:26) To Peter he said,

" . . .When you were younger, you used to fasten your own belt and go wherever you wished. But when you grow old, you will stretch out your hands, and someone else will fasten a belt around you and take you where you do not wish to go." John 21:18

As a chaplain, I once called on a man named Bill in a second rate nursing home. Bill was an alcoholic. He called me "Father Bob." He needed a friend. And the Holy Spirit helped me find one for him. Sam, a recovering alcoholic, invited Bill to his home for Thanksgiving and Christmas. When it came time for Bill to leave the nursing home, Sam made the arrangements. A new home with all the furnishings.

Sam loved the Lord. He also loved Bill. One of the greatest thrills of my ministry was the day Bill called me. "How can I ever thank you for all you did to help?" All I did was introduce Bill to Sam. "Is there anybody you know who might need my help?" he said. He had been loved. Now he wanted to share it.

How many friends have helped me on my faith journey! Pastors, teachers, family members. I am indebted to them. I am now 80 years old. Is it possible for me to offer an encouraging word to someone? So many people live in isolation and they become cynical and depressed. Because we have been loved by Christ, we must feel some compulsion to share it with others. Is there any name that the Holy Spirit might prompt you to call today? Remember how Sam helped Bill.

PRAYER:

Gracious God, I am frail, fragile, and flawed. Please help me to be more sensitive to the many friends who may be lonely, or depressed. Amen.

THE OTHER HALF SERVES GOD

by Rev. Ruben A. Pedersen

(Witness of an African Christian Leprosy Patient)

"Then he said, 'Come no closer! Remove the sandals from your feet, for the place on which you are standing is holy ground.' " Exodus 3:5.

I served as a pastor to the congregation at the Mkalama leper colony, where we had services in a small chapel. At a communion service one day I had an experience I will never forget. One of the worshipers, seated on the bench near   the back, slid from the bench and crawled up to the communion table. As I placed the wafer in the palm of his fingerless hand, with the words, "This is the body of Christ for you," he smiled. I couldn't help but notice his positive outlook on life and his joy, seldom seen in that throng of over 300 colony residents.

I asked him at the close of the service, "How do you account for the joy you seem to have?" Then he told me about his life, how he was driven from his home by his family and found his way to the colony. He continued, "After I arrived here, I had an experience I will not forget. The nurse not only received me and touched me, but proceeded to wash my ulcers. I thought there must be a powerful God who can plant that kind of love in the heart of another person, because there was nothing about me that would encourage such attention. It was a deep concern and love, very unlike the pity and rejection I had experienced elsewhere."

"So I decided to know more about that kind of God. I enrolled in the catechism class, learned about the Savior Jesus Christ, and was baptized. My new name is 'Yohana' (John)." John looked at me, and with deep, emotional conviction, shared his "credo" of life. "I want to be certain that all of the other half of me serves God, as long as I live." I looked at him and I knew what he meant by "the other half." That's about all that was left of him — no fingers, no toes. He had lost one eye. His nasal septum was horribly shrunken. Physically he was a horrible sight, only about "half" of him left. But he wanted to be sure that all of the other half served God. He said, "I will never be able to be an evangelist back home. I'm in this isolated and lonely enclosure, confined here for the rest of my life. I ask God to let me serve him with all that is left."

I left the little chapel that day having heard one of the most powerful sermons of my life! John and I stood on holy ground that day.

PRAYER:

Let us pray: Lord, give us grace to know for certainty that in your presence we are on holy ground, where you call us to praise and serve you with all our being — "all that remains" — for all our days. Amen.

THE GIFT OF HOPE

by Rev. Luther E. Peterson

"How shall we sing the Lord's song in a foreign land?"
Psalms 137:4.

It all began six months ago, in September of 1996. My physician was treating me for walking pneumonia. A chest x- ray revealed a very enlarged heart. An echocardiogram followed. I had always thought that it would never happen to me! I had a heart condition! Heart failure! Three weeks later I landed in the hospital with difficulty breathing. I haven't worked since. I went on disability retirement one year early.

Shortly after that I was put on the list for a heart transplant at the Mayo Clinic. One day I ran across Psalm 137 again. This time it hit me with new meaning (as have many Bible verses lately). "How can I sing the Lord's song in a foreign land?" I had suddenly been thrust unwillingly, kicking and screaming, into a foreign land. Into exile. Or as the King James version puts it, a "strange land." And I too was finding it very difficult to sing the Lord's song.

Psalm 137 begins, "By the rivers of Babylon — there we sat down and there we wept when we remembered Zion." (v. 1) I too learned to cry again as never before. But I have learned to *sing* again, too! Now I anticipate a new adventure ahead with great possibilities — for better understanding others who have suffered unexpected reversals of health or fortune. Also new adventures in reading, writing, and possible future church work as I get a transplant and get stronger again. New adventures that only God knows lie ahead. A time to live in God's promises as never before!

I still cry once in a while. But the peace that comes with this trust is remarkable, and it puts a new "song in our hearts!"

PRAYER:

O God, help us to not allow reversals of health or fortune to devastate us. Give us the gift of faith again today. And give us the gift of hope that makes it possible to get on with our lives with renewed confidence. In Christ's name we pray. Amen.

THE LORD IS MY LIGHT

by Rev. Nelson F. Preus

"The Lord is my light and my salvation; whom shall I fear? The Lord is the stronghold of my life, of whom shall I be afraid?" Psalm 27:1.

The light of God shines into our lives from every page of Scripture, through every hour of our days, even the darkest one. Sometimes that light shines in unusual ways. The design of Olivet Lutheran Church in Fargo, North Dakota, was created to reflect the sturdy quality of "giants in the earth" who settled the Dakota prairies. Cylindrical windows were fashioned from different sized field tile, cut the thickness of the wall and glazed on the outside with storm glass and on the inside with stained glass — not a single pane of round glass, but broken pieces of various colors melded by lead. One piece of glass might break with the build-up of heat in the small enclosure, but the melded stained glass pieces can withstand the pressure of extreme temperatures.

How like those varied windows we are! All of us broken in so many ways, by sin and suffering, disappointment and failure, sorrow and despair. We regret the mistakes of yesterday, dread the uncertainties of today, and fear the unknown future. Like the psalmist, we are surrounded by enemies of all kinds that threaten and terrify us. Into the misery and fearfulness of human life God's penetrating light shines with the power of a laser to dispel fear and free us from the shadows of bondage.

This verse from Psalm 27 has its parallel in John's Gospel where Jesus proclaims, "I am the light of the world, whoever follows me will not walk in darkness, but will have the light of life." (8:2)

We can be confident. The Lord is light, salvation and stronghold, and we, like the windows of the church, are no longer broken but whole, no longer fearful but comforted, held securely in the refuge of God's love.

PRAYER:

O Lord our God, you have commanded the light to shine out of darkness. Forgive me when I have shut my heart to your healing light. Let your light shine so brightly on me that I reflect it to everyone. In Jesus' name. Amen.

THE DITCH

by Rev. Roger E. Raebel

"Call on me in the day of trouble; I will deliver you, and you shall glorify me." Psalm 50:15

"The Lord is near to all who call upon him, to all who call on him in truth." Psalm 145:18

These two passages of scripture have become very meaningful for me from the seventh year of my public ministry. The Lord knew well how important these salutary words were to me on a Spring day in 1962, during my ministry at Grace Lutheran Church, Eldorado, Kansas. Some construction work was being done around the property of our quaint, framed chapel-like building at the corner of Atchison and Pine. A deep trench had been made around the property, in order to lay new water pipes and tile. Barricades were around the construction area for a period of time, and it was necessary that the congregation make use of temporary quarters at a school for our worship services.

In the early part of the construction work, a lady had experienced a sorrow in the death of her husband. She had been laboring with this bereavement for some time. One Sunday morning, as she drove into the area of the trench, not remembering our temporary arrangements for services, she finally found the congregation in worship at the school. Greeting me at the door at the close of the service she said, "Pastor, when I saw that ditch I felt like driving into it." She was distraught, though we had been comforting and counseling her in a number of visits at her home. How did these passages take on such significance for me?

The very next day I was called by her daughter who told me her mother had died during the night. This brief phone call quickly brought to mind words from a hymn . . . "Never safe, except with Thee, Thou my Friend and Guardian be." That day, colloquially speaking, it seems that from a "ditch" I found myself calling upon the Lord. From that point on, these gracious words from the Psalms have been an inspiration to me, and have frequently driven me to my knees, because I have found the Lord faithful to his promises. Call upon the Lord, in need or in daily habit as I do, and you shall surely know the grace of Christ as Savior and God. Unworthy as I am, the Lord has been good to me. Your experience should be no different, if calling upon the Lord in truth.

PRAYER:

Gracious God and Father, in the midst of my trouble or in good days, I thank you for your gracious invitation to draw unto you and to call upon you. Thank you for the gift of the Holy Spirit's indwelling and his ready assistance in making my needs and desires known to you through prayer. Look not upon my unworthiness, due to my sins; but look upon me with eyes of mercy, beholding in me the righteousness of your only begotten Son in whom I believe for forgiveness of sin, life, and salvation. What I ask, I ask in Jesus' name. Accompany me, Lord, at all times, with the right hand of your righteousness, that I faint not in time of trial and am always ready to praise you for your mighty interventions to assist me in my daily life. Lord, look not alone on me, but on others for whom I pray in times of their adversities. Mercifully look upon them in their needs and answer even before they themselves may call upon you. Hear my petition for Jesus' sake. Amen.

AN ORDINARY DAY,
WITH ORDINARY PEOPLE

by Rev. Howard F. Rand

"See what love the Father has given us, that we should be called children of God . . . when he is revealed, we will be like him, for we will see him as he is. And all who have this hope in him purify themselves, just as he is pure."
I John 3:1-3.

In the third act of Thornton Wilder's drama, *Our Town*, 26-year-old Emily has died while giving birth. Before she joins the other departed spirits in the cemetery overlooking Grovers Corners, she asks the Stage Manager if she can return to her town for just one day. She chooses to relive her twelfth birthday. But the pain of seeing what she did not see before becomes ever more poignant.

"Oh, Mama," Emily cries. "just look at me one minute as though you really saw me. Mama, fourteen years have gone by. I'm dead. Just for a moment, we're all together. Just for a moment we're all happy. Let's look at one another." She then cries out to the Stage Manager, "I can't go on. It goes so fast. We don't have time to look at one another. I didn't realize."

"Good-by Grovers Corners...Mama and Papa. Goodby to Mama's food and coffee...to clocks ticking...to sleeping and waking up. Oh earth, you're too wonderful for anybody to realize you." She asks the Stage Manager, through her tears, this awesome question: "Do any human beings ever realize life while they live it — every, every minute?"

An ordinary day. With ordinary people. Lord, how many miracles go unnoticed? We take so much for granted. Jesus Christ could be in our midst. We could miss him completely.

Jesus Christ is in our midst. How do we overcome the familiar? The radical invitation of our Lord is, "Repent! Turn around. Be here now."

A professional religious person spends life telling of holy matters, as if these were our stock in trade. How easily we become underwhelmed by the daily-ness of it all! We may miss the point. I celebrate an ordinary day, with ordinary people.

I remember walking home from my church office for lunch. George was sitting on his front porch. I gratefully stopped to talk. I had never expected George to be so easily relaxing on his porch again. For I had stood by, praying with George in the hospital, wondering if he could hear, waiting sadly with the family for his death to come. The quality of that conversation came not from details of his near-death experience. For mostly it was quite a common conversation. Yet on that mild, pungent fall day, the leaves were giving off a golden glow. I remember his quiet sense of hope.

Charlie came along on his bike. He stopped, chatted in his own, glad-to-be-alive way, the same positive spirit he offered even after his stroke. That very night George was taken by ambulance to the hospital with his last heart attack. It was an ordinary day, with ordinary people. Yet I realized the eternal dimension. A be-here-now moment. There is probably far more to each day than we see.

A pastor is an extraordinarily privileged person. So is every baptized Christian: "See what love; we are God's children now; it does not yet appear what we shall be; we know that when Christ appears, we shall see him as he is."

PRAYER:

A thousand gifts thou dost impart. One more I ask, O Lord: A grateful, thankful heart. Amen.

MORE THAN CONQUERORS

by Rev. Lawrence E. Reyelts

"No, in all these things we are more than conquerors, through him who loved us." Romans 8:37.

I read Romans chapter eight, verses 31 through 39 at the funeral of a pastor of the Lutheran Church in America. It was my privilege to represent The American Lutheran Church by presenting my/our greeting at the celebration of the life of this man whom I had admired.

My brief message pointed out that the words the minister had shared at the bed of many an ill person now were shared to comfort and motivate his family, congregation and all who heard or read them. The fact that we have heard or read these words before does not make them less true. They are empowering, life-setting.

"I can do all things through him who strengthens me," (Philippians 4:13) has not only been my personal theme verse but also has let me ask, take a "no" and ask again.

PRAYER:

Good God, help us to experience your power in our lives. In the name of Jesus Christ we pray, thanking you for him. Amen.

WE ARE SURROUNDED

by Rev. Robert P. Roth

"Therefore, since we are surrounded by so great a cloud of witnesses, let us also lay aside every weight and the sin that clings so closely, and let us run with perseverance the race that is set before us, looking to Jesus the pioneer and perfecter of our faith, who for the sake of the joy that was set before him endured the cross, disregarding its shame, and has taken his seat at the right hand of the throne of God." Hebrews 12:1-2.

The author of Hebrews embraces the full span of time — past, present, and future. Time, like space, is the gift of God in creation. Just as we identify ourselves by finding our place in space, so we know who we are by counting our years in time. We run our race in the present, always supported by those who have gone before us as we reach for the goal that is ahead of us. Hurdles get in our way. Disagreements divide us. Sickness slackens us. But remembrance of the past, the witness of Abraham and Moses, Isaiah and Jeremiah, Luther and Muhlenberg, these great saints together with our own forefathers give us courage and strength to persevere. And Jesus has gone ahead into the future like a pioneer to make our trail perfect so that we can run with speed and without hindrance.

When we are in our twenties, we run full speed in the present. We tend to take the past for granted and immediate gratification precludes proper concern for the future. We need to be admonished about the fullness of time. We need to cultivate gratitude for our parents who have nurtured us in the faith that gives us a foundation for our lives. We need to stimulate imagination to lift us ahead and beyond present concerns.

When we are in our seventies, we tend to lose interest in the future and become lost in the past. If it is true that when we are twenty the possibility of death does not occur to us, when we are seventy we become preoccupied with its inevitability. We need to keep running in the present even though the hurdles are higher, and we need to project our hopes beyond this life to our risen Lord in heaven.

We have so much to be thankful for in the Church. It is true, as detractors say, that religion is responsible for much that is disastrous in history and in personal lives. They point to the Crusades, the Inquisition, the drag on scientific advancement, the Jonestown suicides, the slick deception and hypocrisy of some televangelists. We should learn from these mistakes. But we can also bear witness to the grace of God through the faith of prophets and missionaries, the creativity of architects and artists, the service of pastors and deacons.

All these blessings we owe to Jesus, who died on the cross that we might live. Jesus is our Savior, Lord, and King. We worship him now because 2,000 years ago he died, then rose for us. He promised to come again to shape our future destiny.

PRAYER:

Our gracious Heavenly Father, we thank you for the gift of all the saints who have borne witness to your Son, our Lord Jesus Christ. Give us strength to persevere in the present and hope to lift us into the future. We run the race for Jesus' sake. Amen.

GIVE IT TO GOD

by Rev. Kenneth Roufs

"The Lord will fight for you, and you have only to keep still." Exodus 14:14.

In matters of faith, Pharaoh just didn't get it. The Ten Plagues that struck terror among the Egyptians didn't keep him from pursuing the freed slaves. His hardened heart against Yaweh and Israel brought much confusion and consternation among the people of God. You can be sure questions like, "What's the use," or "Why go on?" filled the camp of Israel. Sometimes, God's people today just don't get it and ask similar questions.

Our Redeeming God chose to be on Israel's side and to keep the plans and promises he previously made and presently intended to fulfil. That's pure grace, the kind best demonstrated for us in Jesus. Knowing their frustrations and their fears, God through Moses made it clear that they should leave their big problem up to him. Thus: *"The Lord will fight for you, and you have only to keep still."* Many times in my ministry I have found assurance and relief personally and with others in trusting the promise the Lord makes in this verse.

I think of Tom, whose ear problems plagued him with aggravating noise and agonizing pain. Whatever his problem was, it baffled the doctors. They tried many things. One time when he mentioned how excruciating his pain had been through the night, I suggested what I had done in difficult circumstances: "Give it to God!" — similar to what Moses and Israel had done — even with some hesitation. But, that's faith!

174

A few weeks later, Tom eagerly sought me out. He said, "I did what you suggested. I gave it to God. I'm not so obsessed with fears about my condition, and consequently I feel so much better." Thank God! When we take him at his word, he lifts the burdens and removes the fears. Why not "give it to God!" He truly cares!

PRAYER:

Gracious and loving God, teach me to trust you for forgiveness in Jesus but also for each day, no matter what. Like Moses, enable me to inspire others to give you their problems. In Jesus' name. Amen.

THE POWER OF WEAKNESS

by Rev. Alvin C. Rueter

"But he said to me, 'My grace is sufficient for you, for power is made perfect in weakness.' . . . For whenever I am weak, then I am strong." 2 Corinthians 12:9-10.

Our daughter Polly was born with only half of her heart developed. Her lips were blue. So were her fingernails. When she was two, the Mayo Clinic marked her chest with a scar, sign of a skillful and merciful deed, the surgeon replacing her aorta with an artery from her leg, prolonging her life until she was seven. The most she ever weighed was 34 pounds.

She and I had a little game; I promised her a quarter when she reached 35 pounds, and she'd always giggle every morning when she stepped on the scale. She never made it. One day while she was still alive, my wife Beulah told me she had seen the neighbor children fighting and that Polly had stepped between them and made them stop. She was so frail they didn't dare resist her.

In my personal relationships and in my ministry, there have been times when I thought I had to be strong, to be tough, to be all-knowing. But it always would lead to pain, and the pain was hardly ever redemptive. I'm gradually learning what Polly taught me — that I don't have to pretend I know everything, that I don't have to pretend I don't hurt, that I don't have to pretend I'm perfect, that the only way I can make it is by grace, that there is power in weakness.

PRAYER:

*As I survey your wondrous cross, O Prince of Glory, help
me to pour contempt on all pride in my own strength and
to grow in your power made perfect in my weakness.
Amen.*

THE PEACE AND THE POWER

by Rev. Russell Sanoden

"Even though I walk through the darkest valley, I fear no evil; for you are with me; your rod and your staff — they comfort me."   Psalm 23:4

I served in the infantry in France and Germany during World War II. I was terribly afraid at first, but one day Christ lifted much of that fear from me. I promised God I would become a pastor. Often we were in deep danger. On Jan 19, 1945, Gus Stavros, a Lutheran now living in St. Petersburg, Florida, went on a patrol in my place. The patrol leader was killed and all of the other soldiers, except one, were wounded, including Gus. What a gift he gave me! Gus later became an outstanding business man and teacher.

While I served with the walking infantry in Europe, Shigeru Nakatta, a Japanese pilot, was serving in the Japanese air force. Twice he nearly lost his life, but escaped both times. Shigeru's last assignment was to fly a small Kamikaze plane loaded with bombs directly into an American warship and blow it up. He did not refuse. Four days before Shigeru was to give up his life the war ended. Can you imagine how he felt?

Shigeru found Christ shortly afterward and married Seiko, who was also baptized. They both went to work for Seiko's father and they lived in the company building. Shigeru was highly successful and a boon to the company. He and Seiko raised two children and are very active in our Lutheran churches.

Shigeru and I met in the 1950's and became warm friends, but we never shared our war experiences with each other until 30 years later, in retirement. Our Lord carried both of us safely through the hell of war in two different nations. We will never cease to thank our God.

PRAYER:

Dear Lord, we thank you for Jesus and the peace and power he puts into our hearts in times of fear. We pray especially for those now torn by war and aggression around our world today. May they find the peace and hope of Jesus through the Holy Spirit. May our world know peace. Amen.

GOD HAS HIS REASONS

by Rev. Albert G. Schilling

"You did not choose me, but I chose you. And I appointed you to go and bear fruit, fruit that will last, so that the Father will give you whatever you ask him in my name. I am giving you these commands so that you may love one another." John 15:16-17

"We know that all things work together for good for those who love God, who are called according to his purpose. For those whom he foreknew he also predestined to be conformed to the image of his Son, in order that he might be the firstborn within a large family. And those whom he predestined he also called; and those whom he called he also justified; and those whom he justified he also glorified. What then are we to say about these things? If God is for us, who is against us?" Romans 8:28-31

Those two portions of scripture have much to say. But I believe they express the central meaning that involves my life, that finally developed in being called into the ministry. And also that God had a purpose as he worked through me. I have experienced many times how God carried out his purpose, and always at the right time. Sometimes we may wonder why God allows certain things to happen in our lives, to us personally. At the time, they seem such a tragedy, and in our eyes or thinking, they seem to hinder our purpose in life as we see it. But often what we may deem a misfortune may be a blessing in disguise, not only for us personally but for others as God works through us later on for the benefit and blessing of someone else.

I had always wanted to be in the ministry of Christ, from childhood. I graduated from a Lutheran academy, but when the depression came in the 1930's

I was not able to continue my education. As time went on, that desire never left me. I remember that I often asked God why he put this desire in my heart for the ministry, but did not make it possible to materialize. However, in 1947 God led me to the seminary, when I had my family.

God had his reasons. The business experience I received during the years of waiting became a blessing for me in my recovery from a heart attack. Because of my business experience, I received a call to another congregation as a business administrator. This was a blessing in my recovery.

And my recovery from a heart attack gave a member of this congregation a new attitude, that one would not necessarily die because one had had a heart attack.

PRAYER:

Lord, may we always realize how important we are at your hand, and what blessing and joy you bestow upon us. Help us to know that we have a wonderful and useful part in your kingdom. You lift us to a higher and nobler level of living through the working power of the Holy Spirit. Thank you, Lord. Amen.

MAKING DISCIPLES

by Rev. Norman W. Schramm

"Go therefore and make disciples of all nations, baptizing them in the name of the Father and of the Son and of the Holy Spirit, and teaching them to obey everything that I have commanded you. And remember, I am with you always, to the end of the age." Matthew 28:19-20.

The graciousness of God is evident in our daily living. God provides. He richly and daily provides for our life and living. God is merciful. He gives us forgiveness and the certain hope of eternal life.

We respond to our Lord's gracious care in various ways. We offer our thanks in daily worship and prayer. Another way to respond to our Lord's graciousness is to faithfully do the work that he has given us to do.

At the time of my ordination, one of the older pastors spoke a blessing in the words from Matthew 28:19. "Go, and make disciples of all people, baptizing them in the name of the Father, the Son and the Holy Spirit, and teaching them to do everything I have commanded you. And remember, I am with you always till the end of the world."

This is a word of God that gave direction to my life and my service to God and fellow persons. Reaching to those who did not indicate a faith in Jesus was always an important part of my ministry. It was evident that some persons did not respond positively to the Gospel of Jesus. However, there were numerous examples that the Gospel is the power of God unto salvation.

A couple had emigrated to the United States. Neither the parents nor their child gave any evidence that they knew Jesus Christ. The opportunity to share Jesus with them became available. It seemed as though all the words may have fallen on indifferent hearts. However, the good seed of the word sprouted, took root and began to grow. The promise, "I am with you," was being realized. After searching the scriptures with them they asked, "Can we be baptized?" The Lord used his word to make these people his disciples. Confessing their faith, they (the parents) and two children were baptized.

What joy was expressed in their lives! They knew and believed in Jesus the Savior. They have continued in the faithful confession of their faith through their daily living, worship life and sharing their faith with others. We rejoice to have experienced again and again that there is a gracious power in God's word. There is a grace and mercy given through that word. And there are thankful hearts because that word is shared. "Make Disciples."

PRAYER:

O God, all good things come from you. You give your grace and mercy to those who look to you in trust and faith. We ask that you would bless all your people that they may share the good news of Jesus that many more may become your followers, your disciples. In the name of Jesus we pray. Amen.

LOVE VS. FEAR

by Rev. James L. Shiell

"Even though I walk through the darkest valley, I fear no evil; for you are with me; your rod and your staff — they comfort me." Psalm 23:4.

"There is no fear in love, but perfect love casts out fear." I John 4 :18.

My battalion commander made an unusual request while I was serving as an Army Chaplain in Vietnam. He told me that no one was willing to disarm a soldier who had just arrived from the States. The young man did not want to be in Vietnam, as if any of us did, and he held a switchblade knife in his hand. Everyone seemed to be gripped by fear as he threatened to attack anyone who advanced toward him. We all faced enough fear and uncertainty in a war zone without having to fear for our own safety in the barracks area.

Why would they ask the Chaplain to do what no one else seemed willing to do? Yet the commander asked me if I would try to talk some sense into this person. What a challenge for me! So I went to the barracks area and had everyone else stay away from him. I maintained a safe distance, making sure he knew I was the Chaplain. I told him I would see to it that no harm would come to him if he gave up his knife to me.

Slowly I moved closer to him as I continued to talk to him and to ask him to *please* give me his knife. While the time seemed to last forever I was finally directly in front of him. He seemed paralyzed by fear and never did give his knife to me. However, he did allow me to take the knife from his hand and I got him to sit down. The immediate crisis was over.

The commander was happy and everyone went on with their work. The soldier received medical attention and probably was sent back to the States for further evaluation. Fear was in all our hearts, fear for our safety was present in the frightened soldier, the commander, everyone involved including myself. Yes, I believe God was with me; with all of us despite all the different circumstances.

There was enough hurt and grief going on in daily events in a war zone without this incident, but that is the way life is for all of us. We thank God for each day and ask for his love and strength no matter what happens.

PRAYER:

Lord, give us your love and strength so that fear does not dominate our lives nor cause us to be paralyzed by our circumstances. Lord, live in our hearts so that your love overcomes our fear. Amen.

THE MIRACLE OF HEALING

by Rev. Arthur M. Solberg

"So let us not grow weary in doing what is right, for we will reap at harvest-time, if we do not give up. So then, whenever we have an opportunity, let us work for the good of all, and especially for those of the family of faith."
Galatians 6:9-10.

In my first parish, I met several persons who were struggling with chemical dependency and the problems that it created in family relationships at . home and at work.

As a result, I enrolled in a chemical treatment center hoping to understand and help those afflicted with the disease. I was also attracted to the program because of the spiritual emphasis.

One of the books used was entitled, *Sobriety and Beyond* by Father John Doe. He asks, "What is spiritual in the AA program?" He replies, "It is all spiritual." Father Doe defines the spiritual person as "one who gets the guidance, strength and help from God through humble prayer and meditation."

He continues to ask, "What can happen if we take the spiritual side of the program seriously?" He replies, "Lives are changed."

I received a letter from a friend in the program while I served one of my parishes. The message reads in part:

"I just happened to think of you around Christmas time, and I was moved to locate you. Many years ago, you and I took a walk down by the lake.

Eventually, I completed my education, enrolled in a seminary, and I am now a pastor in the ELCA."

"As you can see from the enclosed letter, God has blessed us in many ways. As I reflected on where he has led us over the years, you came to mind and I just want to thank you."

Since my retirement I find myself thinking of the many instances in which God brought about his miracle of faith and healing.

Following is a prayer written by another "changed person" as it speaks to her faith:

PRAYER:

Dear God, I have so much to learn about myself and others. Help me to see the things I need to change. Let me be humble enough to ask for the help I need. Release my turmoil. I want to live in peace! Amen.

POWERFUL TESTIMONIES

by Rev. Morris A. Sorenson, Jr.

*"Blessed be the God and Father of our Lord Jesus Christ,
who has blessed us in Christ with every spiritual blessing
in the heavenly places, just as he chose us in Christ before
the foundation of the world to be holy and blameless before
him in love. He destined us for adoption as his children
through Jesus Christ, according to the good pleasure of his
will, to the praise of his glorious grace that he freely
bestowed on us in the Beloved. In him we have redemption
through his blood, the forgiveness of our trespasses,
according to the riches of his grace that he lavished on us . .
."*
Ephesians 1:3-8.

The Japanese garden is masterful in its simplistic
beauty. For me, the most beautiful is the garden at
Roanji, "Temple of the Dragon's Response," in Kyoto.
The garden was laid out by a master nearly 500 years
ago. It is unchanged and has, through the years,
invited contemplation.

I have visited this garden several times, the last
always more impressive than the one before. I have
contemplated the garden's beauty and reflected on
my life and ministry. On my visits to Roanji, my
thoughts have inevitably led me to a consideration of
my thirteen years of service in Japan. I began my
ministry as a missionary there, and after my return to
the United States I have maintained significant ties
with the Japanese church and with a number of
Japanese Christians.

I remember vividly the first Japanese I was privileged
to baptize. He was a student at Waseda University by
the name of Buntaro Nishimura. He told us of his joy
in hearing and feeling the rain, for it reminded him of

188

God's grace and his baptism in water. I remember the courage of Mrs. Hamada who delayed her own baptism until her husband shared her faith. Through her witness, he soon believed and, together with Mrs. Hamada and their daughter, was baptized in the name of the Triune God.

Mr. Masujima became an important and well respected official of the government. I remember when he was still a student, he confessed in my hearing, "The most important thing to me in life is my faith in Jesus Christ."

It is the grace of the living God that gives significance to the life and witness of those whom the Lord welcomes into his kingdom through baptism.

Grace is the center of faith and life in the Lord Jesus. I am a Christian, a follower of the Lord Jesus, because of what God has done for me. Grace describes the reality that God is actor and we are "acted upon." God is the subject and we are the object. Grace is free and undeserved.

In Paul's great hymn in Ephesians 1, we learn again that grace is the gift of God. We are chosen in Christ. We are redeemed through his blood. Through faith in Jesus Christ, our sins are forgiven. And all of this is of God's unfathomable grace!

PRAYER:

Lord, pour out your grace upon us. Open our ears to see and hear the testimony of Christians all around us. And make us witnesses to the faith and life which we have in Jesus. Amen.

THE NEW COAT

by Rev. Dr. Allan B. Sortland

"You were taught to put away your former way of life, your old self, corrupt and deluded by its lusts, and to be renewed in the spirit of your minds, . . ." Ephesians 4:22-23.

I have an old coat at home. I have a number of them, but I'm thinking especially of *one*, a soft, black corduroy sport coat. Yes, I have replaced it — after my wife told me many times, "You've got to get another coat!"

But still, I haven't thrown that black sport coat away. I like it. It travels well. I've used it as a pillow when riding late night buses on overseas trips. It's really quite comfortable.

Do you have a coat like that? The last time I wore mine I got paint on it. So you'll probably never see it . . . I know I have to throw it away. I also know that if you saw it, you'd want me to get rid of it. But I have enjoyed wearing it.

I think of that coat when reading this letter from Paul to the Ephesians. I read what another man had said about an old coat . . . and sin; and I thought . . . my old black sport coat is like sin! When I'm wearing it, it doesn't seem so bad. It's comfortable, even though I know it doesn't look so great.

That's just the way sin is. When you're in the midst of it, it doesn't seem so bad. In fact, we usually like our sins. We have an uneasy sense about them, but we have become so used to them. Sin seems normal. Maybe it is!

The Gospel of Jesus Christ has a word for you and me. It says: "Get rid of the old coat! Put off your old nature which belongs to your former manner of life!" It says: "If you're in Christ, you've got a *new* coat. Put it on!"

Paul was writing to Christian friends in Asia, people who had heard the gospel and responded. They had found salvation in Christ, but their lives didn't show any of the joy of Christ. They were still trapped in their past. So, Paul said, "Put off your old life, the same as you would an old coat. Put on the new clothes, the new nature, the new person!"

For those of us who have sometimes gotten tired of ourselves, our selfishness, our self-centeredness, what a call that is! We can't do that, can we? No, but that is where Christ comes in. He is our righteousness!

So we are invited . . . No, we're commanded, . . . to put on the new clothes he has furnished, to take on the life he has called us to. Then, by the power of the Holy Spirit our lives will change and will begin to reflect the purpose and love of God. Paul is telling us: "Back off from copying the habits and patterns of the world (they are not ours), back off from those things which have been so unsatisfying."

As you put on the new nature, God's power and spirit will enable you to become the person . . . who, in Christ . . . you really are!

PRAYER:

Help us, Lord, to cast off the habits and choices which have hindered us. Help us to open our hearts and lives to your redeeming presence. Amen.

THE ANTIDOTE TO FEAR

by Rev. Howard Sortland

"There is no fear in love, but perfect love casts out fear."
I John 4:18.

There is a lot of fear in people today. In many homes you may find triple locks on doors. A recent survey revealed that thirty percent of American homes possess one or more guns for protection against intruders. Children are constantly warned against carrying on any conversation with an adult not known to the family. People are afraid to walk to their car in a parking lot at night.

Some fear is the better part of wisdom. However, excessive fear can be debilitating. The Apostle John offers a wonderful antidote to fear — *love.* Accepting the love that God gives us can change our lives from the darkness of fear to the joyous light of his presence.

As a young boy growing up in Fargo, North Dakota, our favorite winter pastime was skating on one of Fargo's fine rinks. My one problem was going home in the dark, because I had to go over a half mile stretch through a swampy, desolate area. My imagination heightened my fears to a terrifying level. One night a special girl whom I had dreamed about skating with (but never dared to ask), suddenly asked *me*! She also asked me to walk her home — and she held *my* hand.

That night I hardly even knew that there was a scary swamp to go through. Love had cast out any hint of fear.

When we hold the hand of our Lord, his love and his presence will make our fears disappear even when we walk through the dark shadowy valley of sickness and sorrow.

PRAYER:

Dear Lord, thank you for your perfect love and care, which casts out all fear. Amen.

EVEN GOOD PEOPLE NEED A SAVIOR

by Rev. Arne B. Sovik

" . . . work out your own salvation with fear and trembling; for it is God who is at work in you . . ." Philippians 2:12.

"Pastor," she said, and her whole form reflected the intensity of her effort to convince me, "Pastor, I wouldn't lie to you because you are my pastor. I'm not like a lot of other people. For half my life, ever since my husband died until I began to come to church, I've been a vegetarian. I've not been a sinner." And she clipped off in rapid country dialect a whole list of sins she had not committed.

It was forty-some years ago, in Taipei, and I was examining the lady for baptism. She was sixty-five, illiterate, neat and attractive in black gown and bound feet. I liked her because in spite of her having to get her ten-year-old grandson to read the catechism to her, and in spite of the reluctance of her aging memory, she had obviously made an effort to learn it. Her Buddhist background meant that she was no stranger to the problem of sin and salvation.

But this perturbed me. She sounded for all the world like the Pharisee in the Temple trying to convince God of his righteousness. It looked as if I would have to put her off until she learned a little more about herself. "Why do you want to be a Christian?" I asked her. "If you are such a good person, what can a savior do for you?" She answered without any hesitation. "Even good people," she said, "even good people need a savior." That was enough for me. She was baptized on Christmas Day. She had grasped two all-important elements in her new faith: that a Christian is called to righteous living, and that even the virtuous will find salvation; not in that human virtue, but in the savior.

PRAYER:

Fill my mind today, O Lord, with those things that are good and that deserve praise; things that are true, noble, right, pure, lovely and honorable; and at the end of the day let me rest in the peace of your forgiveness. Amen.

BE NOT AFRAID

by Rev. John M. Steen

"The earth is the Lord's and all that is in it. . ." Psalm 24:1

The year 2000 A.D. is rapidly approaching. The 21st century! A new millennium. Already some are saying that this millennium will usher in the end of the world.

The July 1997 issue of *Popular Science* magazine tells about two astrophysicists who inform us that, yes, the whole universe is closing down. They say we are now living in the "Stelliferous Era" where the stars are the dominant force. This is supposed to last for 100 trillion years (one trillion seconds ago was 200+ years before Christ). Next comes the "Degenerate Era" (sounds more like the present). Lastly comes the "Black Hole Era." Eventually even this, too, will disappear. (Then what, astrophysicists?)

I have a clear memory of the winter confirmation classes of my youth at St. Paul's Church, Billings Park, Superior, Wisconsin. We met in the church kitchen. The oven door was open and the gas was burning. As we huddled together, Pastor Lewis Olson made the catechism and the Bible "come alive" for us. One lesson I learned well was that with Jesus as my Savior and the Holy Spirit as my Guide, I should have no worries or fears as to what the future might hold. So *what* if the world ends! Better things are in store!

I'm sure the shepherds of old thought the world was coming to a close when on that dark night out in the field near Bethlehem, an angel came to them and the glory of the Lord lit up the area. They were scared. Who wouldn't be frightened? But the angel said: *"Be*

not afraid . . . good news . . . to you is born a Savior . . ."
Luke 2:8-14.

It is so comforting to know that God is still on the throne and that He has "the whole world in His hand" . . . even "you and me, brother/sister."

Yes, *"God is our refuge and strength . . . therefore we will not fear . . ." Psalm 46:1-3. "Behold, God is my salvation; I will trust, and will not be afraid; for the Lord God is my strength and my song, and He has become my salvation."* Isaiah 12:2.

PRAYER:

We thank you, Lord, that we can put our trust in you for the present and for the future. We are grateful that Jesus has gone before to prepare "a place" for us. Amen.

LESSONS FROM THE FARM

by Rev. Hal Stoa

"Thy word is a lamp to my feet and a light to my path."
Psalm 119:105.

I remember with nostalgic fondness my days on our North Dakota farm. Robert Fulghum wrote a book entitled, *All I Need to Know I Learned in Kindergarten.* I would say, "All I need to know I learned on the farm!" I share with you a lesson from my youth.

I was seventeen years old and had recently experienced a renewal of my faith. I was eager to learn from God's word and learn its truths for my life. I was experiencing a deep desire to know His will for my life.

I loved farming and thought that this would be my future but I had just placed my life in God's control. What did God have as a plan for my life? I had an uncle who always told me I had the forehead of a banker and there was a business career in my future. I had two uncles who were pastors in the Lutheran Church and they modeled a life of "full-time service." I was an above average student and my teachers told me I could do almost anything I would desire to do.

In a sincere desire to know God's will, I took to searching the Scriptures and praying for direction. I even took my New Testament with me on the tractor and read it while doing field work.

One warm summer day I went to disc our idle acres, a simple and often boring task. This would be a good time to read from the word. I made a couple of rounds and then began to read. Suddenly I became aware of my father's voice over the din of the tractor engine. I looked up to see him frantically waving and calling to me. I glanced behind me and immediately saw the problem. I had been so engrossed in my reading that I had not been steering. I was wandering across the field and making a mess of my work.

My father's words were sharp and to the point. "If you are going to do a good job, you find a target, set your goal and drive straight. Remember, never be distracted, not even by good things."

I heard those words as words from my Heavenly Father. I prayed, decided to set a goal for service in the church and never wavered from that purpose. Thirty-seven years later and recently retired, I realize what a life-changing event occurred that day in a farm field.

PRAYER:

Dear God, give insight in choosing goals of love and service and with our heart fixed on You, may we not waver in living as your child. Amen.

WAIT FOR THE LORD

by Rev. Hal Stoa

" . . . but those who wait for the Lord shall renew their strength, they shall mount up with wings like eagles, they shall run and not be weary, they shall walk and not faint."
Isaiah 40:31

I write this as I sit in a hospital waiting room. My wife is scheduled for five hours of major surgery for a spine condition. My task is to wait, and pray. I discover it is not an easy task to wait. For 37 years I have been a pastor, a helper, a comforter of others. I am used to action, to doing, to being involved in meeting needs. Today I wait. The doctors, surgeons, nurses, and others are in charge. I learn these lessons about waiting:

    Waiting is frustrating as I have so little to do.
    Waiting is humbling as I have no control of events.
    Waiting is lonely even though the room is crowded.   Waiting is slow time. What seems like an hour is
    really only ten minutes!

There is a spiritual lesson here and I hope I can learn from it. To wait on the Lord is recognition that He is in control. Those who wait for the Lord struggle with patience and frustration because our nature mandates action. To wait on the Lord is an exercise in faith and trust. Waiting may be slow time, but it is also a time of renewal.

In the hospital I wait for my wife and reflect on our relationship. I am aware of her precious love, how important she is in my life, how much I need her.

200

Waiting for the Lord is a time of reflection, a time for repentance, a time for renewal of commitment. I remember His love for me, and His lordship of my life. I relax in his power and presence.

PRAYER:

Lord, teach me the lesson of waiting. In the hurry of this day and the rush of events, in the demands of life, help me find space for waiting, praying and renewal. Amen.

SAVING OR SPENDING?

by Dr. Olaf K. Storaasli

"Then Jesus told his disciples, 'If any want to become my followers, let them deny themselves and take up their cross and follow me.' " Matthew 16:24.

Our Lord said that the person who tried to protect or hoard his/her life would inevitably lose it, but the person who was ready to spend his/her life with a kind of prodigal and reckless abandon would find and keep it!

Most of us have learned in our ministries that, as someone has said, there are three kinds of people: those who *make things happen*, those who *watch things happen*, and those who sit back and *ask, "What happened?"*

Our ministries have given us the opportunity to let the Holy Spirit make things happen as the gospel was faithfully preached and taught, and the sacraments were administered. Always, of course, there was the temptation to only watch things happen, or even to sit back and ask, "What happened?" But we do understand that God is not a conception but a living person, and to meet him is to experience him. To have experienced his love and forgiveness, new life, and hope, means that we look upon our fellow humans with love and forgiveness, as well as hope. To constantly receive and not to share is to ignore the *great commandment*, to love our neighbor. There is no sin as ugly as ingratitude.

As an old proverb puts it, "Three things come not back — the spent arrow, the spoken word, and the lost opportunity." Looking back over our ministries, we see many lost opportunities — and that saddens us. But to have been given the privilege to have preached the good news for over 50 years gives us joy and hope because of the promise, "My Word shall not return void." We are thankful that God has given us the opportunity to declare and teach his mercy and grace for these many years, and we are confident that in time "He will bring forth the increase."

PRAYER:

We thank you, Lord, for past opportunities to show and witness to your faithfulness, and we pray that you will continue to speak today through your Good News. Amen.

NEW LIFE FOR OLD

by Dr. Olaf K. Storaasli

"Jesus answered him, 'Very truly, I tell you, no one can see the Kingdom of God without being born from above.'"
John 3:3.

It was a cold, stormy Canadian winter night. Suddenly the doorbell rang and I heard someone stamping his feet on the front steps. Opening the door, I recognized the large man in his fluffy buffalo coat with the upright collar covering most of his head and face. When invited to come in, he abruptly said, "Nicodemus once came to Jesus at night to ask a question. I come by night, too, because I have a burning question."

Like Nicodemus, the man was an influential religious leader. But even such are not exempt from spiritual problems and questions. As Nicodemus was confronted by Jesus with the words, "Unless one is born anew, one cannot see the Kingdom of God," so this respected congregational leader was led from his doubt to see that only in repentance and forgiveness through our Savior, Jesus Christ, can anyone stand upright before him. Of course, like Nicodemus, he asked, "How can this be?" and again the Holy Spirit used the word of promise to lead this troubled, seeking soul to faith and assurance in the atoning work of Christ.

If only more people today would be as honest as Nicodemus was, ask the serious questions regarding forgiveness, and as a result find faith in the "Lamb of God who takes away the sins of the world!"

This seeker, almost physically frozen by the winds of the blizzard (but also spiritually frozen by the formalism in his church), like John Wesley was "strangely warmed" in his heart when he heard the gospel, and confessed his faith in the one whom he now knew was *"wounded for our transgressions, crushed for our iniquities" (Isaiah 53:5).* Yes, one can be born again even when he is old, as Nicodemus also found. Thanks be to God for the Good News of Jesus Christ!

PRAYER:

We thank you, Lord Jesus, that you still meet seekers, and point out to them the necessity of a new birth. We pray that our church and its members may be used by the Holy Spirit to point such seekers to the Lamb of God that takes away the sins of the world. Help us to share the good news with such troubled souls — and to each other! Amen.

GIVE IT A TRY

by Rev. Calvin Storley

"Create in me a clean heart, O God, and put a new and right spirit within me. Do not cast me away from your presence, and do not take your Holy Spirit from me. Restore to me the joy of your salvation, and sustain in me a willing spirit." Psalm 51:10-12.

The devotional I suggest to you in the text that follows may take you days, weeks, even months. As Hallesby suggests in his book on prayer, "To pray is to let Jesus come into your heart." Our task and our only task in our devotional life is to make ourselves available, open to God. It is not bringing our list of needs and concerns before Him; it is reporting for duty, awaiting instructions for the day, for life. Prayer is not so much telling God what He already knows better than I; it is spending focused time quietly listening to what God has to say to me.

God speaks in many ways. However, one of the most effective ways is through the scriptures. A classic example is found in Isaiah 6. (Read and meditate upon this chapter). Isaiah lived in turbulent times. His mind and heart were filled to breaking heaviness with the state of affairs among God's people. He went to the temple to pour out his heart before God. How long he stayed we do not know, but it was long enough for him to experience his whole being as it was filled and surrounded with the overwhelming presence of God. Hopelessness and defeat were replaced with cleansing, hope and light. Most of all, the confidence that God was still in charge. Knowing that Isaiah could say, "Here am I — send me," he could go on with his life. That is always the hoped-for result of our devotional life.

Give it a try:

1. Begin each day praying slowly and meditatively. Psalm 51:10-12.
2. Read, meditate on, and memorize one of these passages:

> Matthew 28:19-20; 5:13-16; 6:5-13; 7:7-11.
> Mark 5:1-19 (special focus on v. 19)
> Luke 10:1-2
> John 3:16
> Acts 1:8, 12-14; 4:19-20
> II Timothy 1:7
> I Peter 3:15
> Romans 8:26
> Philippians 4:6-7

> *Ask the following. Be sure to spend time just letting thoughts come as they will. Sit quietly, listen; let God direct.*

> What does the passage say?
> What does it mean for me?
> What will I do about it?

3. Bring your needs and concerns; talk them out with God.
4. Open your hymnal. Read the text of your favorite hymns. Stay with one hymn each week. Note how many are prayers.

PRAYER:

God bless you and keep you; God make His face to shine upon you and be gracious unto you; God lift up His countenance upon you and give you peace. Amen.

A STORM STILLED

by Rev. Luther O. Strommen

"And when he got into the boat, his disciples followed him. A windstorm arose on the sea, so great that the boat was being swamped by the waves; but he was asleep. And they went and woke him up, saying, "Lord, save us! We are perishing!" And he said to them, "Why are you afraid, you of little faith?" Then he got up and rebuked the winds and the sea; and there was a dead calm. They were amazed, saying, "What sort of man is this, that even the winds and the sea obey him?" Matthew 8:23-27

I will never forget the experience of that evening. It was strange and puzzling in many ways. My naiveté, my complete lack of understanding of mental illness, and my childlike faith and confidence in Jesus and His word are all part of the equation.

A member of our church had called and asked me to visit her parents in a motel just outside of town. They were having a problem with her brother, a young man about twenty years old. Unbeknownst to me, he had recently spent time in the Fergus Falls State Mental Hospital. He was determined to go to the local radio station to warn the people to repent and make ready for the day of judgment that was upon them.

When I arrived, we simply sat and talked. They reported what was going on and he, with great agitation, told of his concern and compulsion to act. I read a passage about Jesus stilling the tempest. I spoke briefly of what that meant to me, and led in prayer. Of course, we had coffee. It was time to go.

Again, his agitation broke forth in expression of his conviction of what he must do. Perplexed as to how I should help these dear old people (that's how they seemed to me at my tender age of twenty-six), I made a quick decision. I would spend the night with this young man!

So we went to bed. I was hardly down when he sat upright in his bed announcing his determination to get to the radio station. I responded by retelling the story of Jesus stilling the tempest. He quieted down. Each time he gave vent to his anxiety I began with the story and told it through with emphasis on the winds made still and the waters made quiet. Finally, we both fell asleep. I awakened to slip out to meet the 4 a.m. train.

Later that morning a quiet and rested young man came to the parsonage to thank me. He had just been to his doctor for a new prescription. Only then did I realize that he was on medication. With him he had a copy of Hallesby's devotional opened to the reading for that day. It was beautifully relevant and appropriate.

The storm was over. The psychotic episode was past. He would live to attend LBI and become the father of a pastor named Luther (not Lutheran, however). Like Mary, I have not only remembered but pondered this experience of the power of the word.

PRAYER:

Dear God, Thank you for reminding us that you are not only the King of Creation, but also the Lord of our lives. You have power to still the tempest that so often erupts deep within. Give us the faith to trust you completely , when the solution to our problems seems beyond our reach. Let your word, O Lord, move in with impressive power. Amen.

THE LOST SHEEP

by Rev. Dr. Merton P. Strommen

"What do you think? If a shepherd has a hundred sheep, and one of them has gone astray, does he not leave the ninety-nine on the mountains and go in search of the one that went astray? And if he finds it, truly I tell you, he rejoices over it more than over the ninety-nine that never went astray. So it is not the will of your Father in heaven that one of these little ones should be lost." Matthew 18:12-14.

Let me share a story of how faith was lived out by a layman who went looking for a lost sheep. The lost sheep was my grandfather, Andrew, a hard-working farmer, baptized and confirmed in the Lutheran church, who took a great deal of pride in his physical strength and much pleasure in his hard liquor. Fights because of the latter two were not uncommon.

His brother, Gilbert, living in Fergus Falls, was a devout Christian, deeply concerned about the "lostness" of Andrew. So Gilbert traveled to Blanchardville, Wisconsin, for the express purpose of talking with him about his relationship to God.

My uncle, Clarence, then a twelve-year-old boy, heard their conversation. He was in the bedroom just above the room where Gilbert and Andrew were talking. He could hear everything by listening, with his ear to the hot air register in the floor — and the ceiling above the room where the men were talking.

Gilbert began by expressing concern over his brother's apartness from God. Hearing this, Andrew became angry, swore, and ordered him out of the house. But Gilbert persisted. After a time, Andrew's high decibel voice subsided and their conversation became less threatening. In subdued voices, their conversation continued into the night long after Uncle Clarence had fallen asleep. When he came down for breakfast he heard his father, Andrew, summon the family and announce that the previous evening he had become a Christian. Then he said, "From now on, we, as a family, will begin each day with devotions."

Years later, while interviewing my uncle, I heard him say, "My dad really changed. No, he never preached, he never spoke publicly in church, but it was in our home that we saw the change. He kept his promise about having devotions every day."

Each of us in the Strommen family owe a debt of gratitude to Gilbert for having been the shepherd willing to seek out this lost sheep. The resulting faith of his home has become a legacy we, as a family, enjoy and treasure.

PRAYER:

Gracious Lord, thank you for having found and redeemed me for all time. Help me, in turn, to be an instrument of your Spirit in bringing one who is lost back to you. Impress on me the cosmic significance of the importance of being in a saving relationship with you. Amen.

Concerning The Word

by Rev. Carl C. Sunwall

"I have made your name known to those whom you gave me from the world. They were yours, and you gave them to me, and they have kept your word. Now they know that everything you have given me is from you; for the words that you gave to me I have given to them, and they have received them and know in truth that I came from you; and they have believed that you sent me." John 17:6-8.

In this prayer, Jesus gives us a brief summary of his ministry, and an outline for the ministry of knowledgeable believers. The word is received, known, believed, kept, lived, and shared. The Bible begins with these words, "In the beginning God." The Gospel by John begins with the words, "In the beginning was the word and the word was with God and the word was God." Later we read that, "the word became flesh and dwelt among us." This tells us that God was incarnate in Jesus Christ.

It is Known. As we think of knowing the word, we remember, perhaps most of all, Sunday School, where we were taught the Word, and came to believe it as a means of grace.

It is Believed. *"So faith comes from what is heard, and what is heard comes through the Word of Christ."* Romans 10:17. The word bears its own fruit.

It is Kept. *"Thy word have I laid up in my heart that I might not sin against Thee."* It is memorized to be available for use at all times. Again, Sunday School bears fruit.

It is Lived. Among others there are two words that have a very special meaning for us of faith. These are Righteous and Pious. Righteous is the fruit of the word in our hearts. Pious is the Righteousness being lived.

It is Shared. By thought, word and deed, we give it to others. The word, given, received, known, believed, kept and shared, bears fruit in the hearts and lives of others.

An elderly lady called me long distance recently, to express her appreciation for my sharing the word in Bible Studies and preaching over fifty years ago. She said, "I accepted Jesus as my Savior, through your ministry of sharing the word of God." At a fellowship of retired church staff people last week, a pastor contacted me. I confirmed him fifty-five years ago, as a youth member of the congregation. He expressed his gratitude for my involvement in his father's acceptance of Jesus as his Savior. The word bears fruit for eternal life.

PRAYER:

We thank thee, Lord, for the High Priestly Prayer by Jesus. We thank thee for the reminder for us, of the reception, knowledge, faith, living, and sharing of the word of God. We pray that the word shared in this devotional may be a means of increasing our knowledge and strengthening of our faith. We pray this in the name of the Father, the Son, and the Holy Spirit. Amen.

COMFORT TO GIVE,
COMFORT TO RECEIVE

by Rev. Freeman O. Sveom

" . . . who consoles us in all our affliction, so that we may be able to console those who are in any affliction with the consolation with which we ourselves are consoled by God."

2 Corinthians 1:4.

Hopefully, as one looks back on the years of ministry, it has been a privilege to be able to bring a message of hope and comfort to those who have suffered some of life's unexplainable tragedies. Within the family of God, through Word and Sacrament and personal witness, we seek to bring to hurting souls the comfort which only God can give. We can rejoice with those who rejoice and weep with those who weep. As the gospel is meant to convict and point people to Christ, so the gospel is also a means of bringing healing and consolation. By God's grace, we become vehicles through which others are blest.

By the same token, it is equally true that we become the recipients of that comfort which we have sought to bring to others.

There is a strange reciprocity that prevails among those who claim fellowship with Christ — as one gives, so one receives. That comfort that we seek to reach out to others, we find coming back to us.

It is now twenty-two years since my wife, Ann, suffered a stroke which has left her with an inability to speak and has restricted her communication skills of reading and writing. Naturally, depression and despondency can be present. However, she has, over all these years, reflected a wonderful and gracious spirit.

It has been our privilege over these twenty-two years to be members of three different congregations. In each of these fellowships, it has been a God-given blessing to us to feel the support, understanding, and comfort that has surrounded us. When days have not always been bright, when unanswered questions are ever present, when tomorrow does not always seem clear, we have always found that we are "comforted with the comfort with which we ourselves are comforted by God."

We are deeply grateful to all those within the fellowship of Christ and the church who have comforted us with prayers, love, concern, and Christian comfort.

PRAYER:

Dear God, we thank you for our Lord Jesus, and the grace and mercy which is the source of all our comfort. May we gladly reflect this in our lives and rejoice in the supporting hands and hearts of fellow believers. Amen.

JUST AN ORDINARY CHRISTIAN

by Rev. M. Douglas Swendseid

"But each of us was given grace according to the measure of Christ's gift." Ephesians 4:7.

Sure, I understand that together with all Christians, I am called to serve Christ in this world. But what can I do? I'm a very ordinary Christian. I'm not a leader. I don't have any special training. I'm not in a position of power or authority and besides, my life is already much too busy!

Ephesians 4:7 suggests that we are all gifted persons in Christ even if we do not feel gifted. Often we do not realize how God uses our gifts for God's purposes.

This truth became especially clear to me when I was a staff person in the former ALC National Offices in Minneapolis. A young woman came to our World Mission office to inquire about a two-year English language teaching program in Japan. She was a Lutheran Christian but she had grown up in a secular Jewish home in New York City. Some ten years earlier, as a high school student, she had participated in a summer exchange program. She had gone to rural Wisconsin and lived with a Lutheran family on a dairy farm. The first Sunday after her arrival came and there was no discussion about religion or whether anyone might want to, or not want to, attend worship. In that household everyone went to church on Sunday morning. She, therefore, went also and she went every Sunday during her summer stay. At first, she rather resented having to go to a Christian church service but as the summer went by, in the context of the acceptance, kindness and love of that family, she went willingly. They were the first

Christians she had ever known in any depth and they were not at all like what she had learned about Christians. She did not become a Christian that summer but a little later, in college, she sought out a Lutheran pastor — Lutheran because that Lutheran family represented Christianity to her — and found her way to faith and baptism.

Gifted in the practice of hospitality, this Wisconsin family welcomed the stranger with an open, warm and loving attitude. Through them, our Lord welcomed this young woman and she joined Christ's church and found life eternal!

PRAYER:

Thank you, Lord, for not only calling me into your mission service but also giving me the gifts and means to carry out that service. Help me to remember that I am called to love those whom I meet and with whom I interact, not in word or speech, but in truth and action. Amen.

GOD SEES OUR HEARTS

by Rev. Ralph L. Tellefsen

" . . . what does the Lord require of you but to do justice, and to love kindness, and to walk humbly with your God?"
Micah 6:8.

This illustration is from our congregation, Concordia Lutheran, at Fertile, Minnesota. When conducting funerals, there were occasions where we might question the relationship of the deceased to the Lord. I recognize that God makes the ultimate and correct decision, and we as individuals can make mistakes. We cannot see the heart, as God does.

But as I thought and prayed about this, I shared my concerns in a Sunday morning sermon. I suggested that all of us, in our homes and with our families, should talk about our relationship with the Lord with one another. For example, a husband with his wife, children with their parents. The next Sunday a man came to me and said, "I shared with my wife my personal relationship with the Lord." When death came to him a few weeks later, there was no doubt or uncertainty about his place in heaven and eternal life.

I believe this was a blessing in my ministry and a joyful experience for that entire family. For isn't it true that there is more joy in heaven over one sinner that repents, rather than over ninety and nine righteous persons who need no repentance.

Another visit I'll remember for a long time was at Lyngblomsten Care Center. We were calling on a pastor's wife who had had a stroke. She could no longer speak, but watching her eyes and her expression we knew she understood us. We had called on this pastor and his wife years ago in their

North Dakota parish to ask him to be part of our staff in Crookston. He decided he could not leave his people in his present community. But his wife served us a delicious dinner, with apple pie for dessert. Apple pie is my favorite, and I commented about it.

When we visited her at Lyngblomsten, my wife and a friend tried their best to make some contact through conversation, to no avail. Then I reminded her about the apple pie and how we had appreciated it. She responded with a beautiful smile. Then I began to sing in Norwegian, "Skriv deg Jesus pa mit hjerte, O min konge og min God," and she sang with me until the final Amen. What a wonderful experience to reach a person through song in Jesus our Lord!

This is the message in English: "On my heart imprint thine image, Blessed Jesus, King of Grace, that life's riches, cares and pleasures have no power Thee to efface. This the clear inscription be, Jesus crucified for me, is my life — my hope's foundation, and my glory and salvation."

PRAYER:

Search me, O God, and know my heart; try me and know my anxious thoughts, and see if there be any hurtful way in me. Lead me in the way everlasting. Amen.

THE CLOCK OF LIFE

by Rev. Leonard C. Thaemert

"Be careful then how you live, not as unwise people but as wise, making the most of the time, because the days are evil." Ephesians 5:15-16.

"We have plenty of time," so I thought as I glanced at the clock on the electric stove. It was the most reliable timepiece in the parsonage of a dual parish I had been called to serve in Northern Minnesota. It was a dark, cold, wet Saturday in December, and that evening I was to perform my first marriage in the sister congregation. Repeatedly I glanced at the clock still thinking, "We have plenty of time."

That day, however, an electrician, while correcting a problem, had turned off the electricity for 45 minutes and did not reset the clock. My wife and I left. It was only seven miles, we would be there in plenty of time. But when we arrived there was pandemonium. The bridal party had been nervously waiting in the narthex for a half hour. All this because we did not realize how late it was.

As we look at the clock of life, we are easily tempted to think that we still have plenty of time; time to worship, time to serve the Lord in His church with our time, talents and treasure, time to help our neighbor in need with deeds of love and kindness, time to share our faith and salvation in Christ with others.

Woodworking was my hobby and making grandfather clocks my specialty. I wound and reset many of them. But the clock of life no one can wind or reset. Only God can do that.

And let us always keep in mind that —

The clock of life is wound but once
And no one has the power
To tell just when the clock will stop
At late or early hour.
To lose one's wealth is sad indeed,
To lose one's health is more.
To lose one's soul is such a loss
That no one can restore.
So do not wait until tomorrow to do His blessed will.
The clock of life may then have stopped,
The hands may then be still.

PRAYER:

Lord, teach us to number our days that we may apply our hearts unto wisdom and use the time that You give us to glorify You and serve our fellow man, for the sake of our blessed Savior who gave his all for us. Amen.

SOMETHING THAT NEVER DIES

by Rev. Conrad Thompson

"Jesus Christ is the same yesterday, today and forever."
Hebrews 13:8.

A friend of ours from Norway told a story about a
little boy whose parents gave him a dog. Andy was
proud of that dog. He played with it and soon they
became the best of friends. One day the dog ran
across the street and was killed by a car. What a sad
day this was for Andy! Then, to assuage Andy's
sorrow, his parents gave him a cat. And with equal
fervor he accepted this cat as his playmate and friend.
But one day the cat got sick and died. Again Andy
was devastated and to comfort him his parents gave
him a bird. Day after day he watched this bird as it
fluttered around in its cage. I Ie loved to hear its
songs. But one day the bird flew out of the cage and
in its fear flew against the window so hard that it was
killed. With all of these sad experiences Andy said to
his parents, "Will you give me something that never
dies?"

Lately I have been reading again about our ancestors
coming to this country. Everything was strange to
them. The culture, the political life, the economics and
the virgin land were all different. It was as if their
past had died and was only a memory. Many were
lonely, depressed and wondered why they had come.

But soon after they came they met for worship, first in
their homes and then in humble churches. Here they
discovered they had something that never dies. As
they sang the old hymns — "Behold a host arrayed in
white, like thousand snow clad mountains bright . . ."
and, "Jesus I long for thy blessed communion,
Yearning for thee fills my heart and my mind . . .",

"My hope is built on nothing less than Jesus' blood and righteousness . . ." — they felt connected to the eternal. Here they confessed their sins and were forgiven. Here they confessed their faith in Jesus Christ and sensed that they were in the company of the saints of God everywhere, in heaven and on earth. Here they were assured that Jesus Christ is the same, yesterday, today and forever.

PRAYER:

Lord, as we face sickness, sorrow and the trials and changes of our age, we know that Christ never changes. His grace is sufficient for all things. He promises to supply our every need. No matter what happens, in Christ we have something that never dies. Amen.

LORD, YOU CAN COUNT ON ME

by Rev. Clifton E. Trued

"Then Jesus told his disciples, 'If any want to become my followers, let them deny themselves and take up their cross and follow me.'" Matthew 16:24.

"Commitment" is a big word in our English vocabulary. We all make commitments all the time, probably every day. Some of us have made a marriage commitment and we were asked: "Will you take (this person) to be your wife (husband), to have and to hold . . .?" If so, answer, "I will." It is a promise to the other person. "You can count on me!"

But commitments are sometimes less than honest. Commitments have been known to be lukewarm or half-hearted. I've known a husband for years who has wavered all his married life about his relationship with his wife.

Have you heard the story about the couple who were getting more and more serious about their relationship? On proposal night he said to her, "Honey, I know I can't give you everything that some other men can give you, like Jerome who is rich and has a yacht and drives a Ferrari, but I love you and I want to marry you." And she said, "I love you, too, Honey, but tell me a little bit more about Jerome."

Lots of people enter into a relationship with their fingers crossed, or with divided allegiances. "Tell me a little more about Jerome."

Jesus has promised, "You can count on me!" He demonstrated it in the cross event. He didn't have his fingers crossed; it was not a lukewarm commitment. And he has demonstrated it to the people of faith throughout history and continues to prove it to us in our daily lives. It's a basic plank in our life of faith: We know we can count on Jesus! He walks with us on our daily journeys, upholding, healing, empowering, forgiving us.

He solicits our commitment in return: "Can I count on you?" Sometimes it's a once-and-for-all-time response. Sometimes it's a daily response we make, without fingers crossed, without wavering. "Lord, you can count on me to be faithful, to cherish and deepen our relationship. You can count on me to deny myself, to pick up my cross and follow you."

PRAYER:

Lord, thanks for your commitment to the world you made, for love, and for your personal commitment to us as individuals. Please sustain each one of us in our response: "Lord, you can count on me." Amen.

NEEDS ARE UNDERWRITTEN BY GOD

by Rev. Clifton E. Trued

"Do not fear, for I am with you, do not be afraid, for I am your God; I will strengthen you, I will help you, I will uphold you with my victorious right hand." Isaiah 41:10.

These words were spoken to the nation of Israel; I claim these promises personally.

On a pleasant Sunday afternoon, my wife and I sat relaxing in our living room. She left for a few moments, but barely made it up the stairs when she returned. At the hospital she was diagnosed as having had a heart attack. It changed our lives completely.

The triple by-pass surgery went well — for several days. Then a murmur was detected and an echogram revealed that a hole had appeared in the septum separating the upper heart chambers. More surgery was performed to patch the hole. Recovery went well — for three months. Then another murmur. Thinking the patch had come loose, the surgeon arranged for more surgery to fix the problem, only to discover there was a different hole. So, another patch went into place.

Hemorrhaging was life-threatening and required a return to the operating room to cauterize the bleeding veins. Recovery was slower, but progressed gradually — for three months. Then another murmur and another hole.

At this stage, additional surgery was too risky. The heart was pumping valiantly, trying to supply the various organs and systems with oxygen and other nutrients. It was not succeeding. All this time our family of faith — meaning the congregation I was serving, as well as members of previous congregations I had served and lots of other people — were praying fervently for her healing. The Lord was very present, providing us with strength to meet each crisis and our daily needs.

Our hopes were raised when our cardiologist learned of a doctor in Boston who had invented a device which was inserted through an artery into the heart chambers, expelled an umbrella-like patch on the far side of the septum and then affixed it in place with a reverse-facing umbrella, thereby sealing the hole. The usual procedure took two hours, but after trying valiantly for almost eight hours, the doctor gave up guided only by the flow of blood. He was unable to place the plug in position without interfering with the action of a nearby heart valve. Besides, there was always the possibility of losing the mechanism in the blood stream, which would have created a disastrous situation.

The whole procedure occurred under local anesthetic. What an ordeal! When the doctor came into the waiting room to report the failure, it was like hearing the death sentence. Now it was clear: unless the Lord intervened in a spectacular (miraculous) way, there was no hope. The Lord chose not to intervene. And so, after five years of watching my lovely and loving wife die an inch at a time, the Lord sent his angels to take her home. It was ten days after our Golden Wedding Anniversary.

The bond between us grew stronger throughout the crisis, and our relationship with the Lord deepened. We benefitted from the prayers and ministry of the communion of saints. Our faith in God was always active, and I still claim the gifts of strength, help and support which the Lord promises. It is much easier to walk with others in their crises and pain when we have experienced them ourselves.

PRAYER:

Thanks, O Lord, for your invitation to draw upon all your resources to meet our needs. Thanks for your healing touch of mercy, forgiveness and grace and for your power of healing in the midst of pain.   Amen.

BLESS THE LORD, O MY SOUL

by Rev. Erling M. Tungseth

"Bless the Lord, O my soul, and all that is within me, bless his holy name. Bless the Lord, O my soul, and forget not all his benefits." Psalm 103:1-2.

This Psalm was the focus of my life during March and April of 1997. I had two falls on the ice. Following that, I had two cranial surgeries — one on March 7th and the second on April 3rd. Before both surgeries at Abbott Northwestern Hospital in Minneapolis, my right hand had lost strength and my speech was very limited.

Bless the Lord, O my soul, and forget not all the benefits coming from God. Forgiveness for all iniquities. As far as the east is from the west, so far has God removed our sins from us. He heals all your diseases. I held on to these benefits praying for recovery to my old self.

With a family, including a wife and two teenagers, I was praying that I would have many years to watch them develop. I prayed that my wife and I would see them develop to their independence and careers in life.

I have a ministry as visitation pastor that I love, and I prayed that this would be a reality again. Now I am doing well. I am at home with my family and enjoying my church ministry again. So I am experiencing the benefits of God supplying my needs through a great surgeon and hospital staff, through my family and friends who are praying for me.

PRAYER:

Our Dear Heavenly Father, we thank you for your caring love, your healing power, and for your promise that you are with us always. Bless the Lord, O my soul, in Jesus' name. Amen.

PERFECT GIFTS

by Rev. Carl P. Vaagenes

"Every generous act of giving, with every perfect gift, is from above, coming down from the Father of lights, with whom there is no variation or shadow due to change." James 1:17.

It was July 20, 1986. The surgery and chemotherapy that followed changed the course of my life. I thank God for it all, although the survival prognosis was two years at the most. Through this crisis, God brought me into a new experience of life's spiritual dimension. I thank God for the competent care given by the best of medical professionals, and to this day I bless them for using their God-given talents and skills for good.

At the time my cancer was discovered, I was ready to write my doctoral thesis entitled, "The Gifts of the Holy Spirit in a Lutheran Congregation." The consensus of theologians is that the charismatic gifts operating in the early church are no longer needed. The two reasons given: "We should use the divinely ordained means, both in the realm of nature and of grace" rather than be presumptuous in what we believe; and the Old and New Testament scriptures are sufficient for faith and life. Dogmaticians explained that people through whom miracles occur are extraordinary examples of *"fides heroica."* It was this thesis I was ready to defend. That is, until my encounter with God's supernatural gifts and power which were invoked and applied for my healing.

A new convert in the Tofte parish who had heard of my doctor's verdict asked the Lord how to pray for me and was given Romans 8:11 as a promise for me to claim (which I did). Two others confirmed this promise for me.

So I was moved to restudy all my gathered resources, and I began, as I had done before, with the Bible. In my faith struggle with cancer, I had to deal with my trials as the faith testings spoken of in James 1:2b. When I came to James 1:17, my eyes were opened as never before to God's *two giftings*: "good *endowments*" and "perfect *gifts*." I am still learning much about God's use of our good, natural abilities and His perfect, supernatural gifts.

Even as I thank God for the "good endowments" used by God for my physical healing (which through anointing and prayer provided a miracle) and which "good endowments" are used by God for the Church's ministry and service, I also (and especially) am thanking God for the "perfect gifts," the supernatural gifts of God. It is through the charismatic gifts God edifies open-minded but imperfect believers for their ministry, and it is through His gifts given to Spirit-filled believers that the Church will fulfill Christ's mission of salvation and healing in the power — not of man — but of the Holy Spirit. May we be faithful in our use of God's giftings.

PRAYER:

Lord, may we open our eyes to see the perfect gifts you offer us. Amen.

OUR ORPHANED SAVIOR

by Rev. Thomas W. Wersell

" . . . Woman, here is your son . . . disciple, here is your mother." John 19:26-27.

"Preacher, you're never too old to learn." So said a lecturer to retired clergy. I know what he meant.

For example, I was long gone from the seminary when I had a new learning about those painful words from the Cross. I learned they were not about the fidelity of Jesus towards his mother. Nor were they about John being her comforter when Simeon's prophecy, *" . . . a sword will pierce your own soul . . .",* was experienced.

Those cross words were about sin. Sin embodied in Jesus.
Our sin. "For Christ bore our sins, and not his own, when he on the cross was hanging," wrote Nikolai Grundtvig.

With his words to Mary and John, Jesus severed his dearest earthly connections. Essentially, on the cross he became a crucified orphan. All alone, totally bereft of help from grieving mother or silent father. Forsaken, not as sinner but as sin. On our sin-bearer, the Lord laid all human iniquity from Eden's garden to time's end. The Incarnate Son became incarnate sin. Oh the shame. Oh the horror. Oh the struggle. Oh the loud, "Why?"

Holy wrath turned away from personified sin hanging there abandoned. The solitary Jesus was made a blood offering to save us all.

"There was no other good enough to pay the price of sin." What a Savior! He did it his way, all the way. For me, out of everlasting love. For you. For every believer.

PRAYER:

Lord Jesus, orphaned Savior, you died to save us all and make us children of God, our Father. We thank and praise you. Amen.

RELEASE

by Rev. Clifford M. White

"Create in me a clean heart, O God." *Psalm 51:10*

The following is the story of a powerful experience of
forgiveness by one of the respected members of my
congregation, a man dying of cancer. It is told in
verse and begins with my first hospital visit to him.

I came into the room.
The scene arranged itself.
The women on each side,
The man between in bed,
Flat with swollen belly,
Holding a malted milk.
"He looks so good," they smile.
"Much better every day."
He looked an empty look,
Knowing how they lie,
A scene scented by death,
Wreathed in hollow words,
Trying not to say,
Trying not to see.

But then that other day:
an unexpected call.
"Come," he asked, "can you?"
I go as fast as wind,
Turning, churning inside,
Asking, wondering why,
And come into the room.
He's there, thin arms and all
And bloated belly full.
He tells of a time long gone,
Fifteen years before,
But still with him today,
When, in anger's flame,

He raised an arm of hate
To a boy who ran away.
And how the boy was found
Cold and wet and drowned.
He could not still the pain
That jabbed into his mind,
Nor wipe away the stain of guilt.
He looked to me for help.

I reach out for the book
And simply read the Psalm
Of David's cry of guilt
That's numbered fifty-one.
My voice, soft and flat,
With tongue quivering, dry;
There is no more to do.
There is no more to say.
A word was read and heard.
"Thank you," he said, "that helps."
And so we sat and looked
And knew, though death was there,
A torn life had been healed
By a word of grief and hope.
And nothing more was said.
We simply rested back.
And let its power surround.
Nothing more was said.

PRAYER:

Lord God, open us every day to the renewing power of your forgiving grace, in Jesus' name. Amen.

AN ENCOUNTER WITH A HERO
OF THE FAITH

by Rev. Walter R. Wietzke

St. Paul sets the tone for entering a new year —
" . . . *forgetting what lies behind . . . I press on toward the
goal for the prize of the heavenly call of God in Christ
Jesus." Philippians 3:13-14.*

Back in the 1940's, as a seminary student in
Columbus, Ohio, I saw a movie, *Pastor Hall,* dealing
with the resistance of the German church to Naziism.
It was at least a veiled reference to people like Martin
Niemöller, a confessed Christian, who had become
Hitler's personal prisoner. I was captivated with the
thought, "What would it be like to meet a man like
that?"

Thirty years later, now pastor of University Lutheran
Church in East Lansing, Michigan, I received a phone
call from a friend in the National Lutheran Council
office in New York. "Walt, can you do us a favor?
We'd like you to host a visitor for three days and set
up a series of lectures and meetings with faculty and
students at Michigan State University. Can you
handle it?"

"Yes. Who is the visitor?"

"Martin Niemöller."

Those three days and nights led to a fine relationship.
And it was so easy. He was the spitting image of my
maternal grandfather, wore the same kind of shoes,
smoked the same cigars, had the same facial features,
mustache and all.

When the sessions were ended I drove him to the home of his daughter in Ann Arbor. Anxious to satisfy my own curiosity, I asked, "Did you ever actually encounter Hitler?" He paused, then with a hint of a smile answered, "Once, only once, but it was memorable!" Pastor Niemöller, the point man in the resistance movement, defying the conqueror of Europe, the tyrant who triggered World War II. "But Valter," he concluded, "I never think about those times; they are only like a bad dream. My thoughts are on this generation and what will happen tomorrow, how these young people are affected by atheism and secularism. What Jesus means for them is my concern," which was his theme in every session.

PRAYER:

So we pray, Lord, help us to start this year "forgetting what lies behind," pressing on to the future, concerned with the coming generation, with what Jesus means for them — and for us. Amen.

THANK YOU, SAINTS

by Rev. Griffith H. Williams

"To all God's beloved in Rome, who are called to be saints: Grace to you and peace from God our Father and the Lord Jesus Christ." Romans 1:7-8.

You and I can learn a lot from the most famous of God's saints — those heroes and heroines of the faith whose lives were so exemplary and whose accomplishments so notable that they are known throughout the world on a first name basis. You know the ones I mean: St. Paul, St. John, St. Peter and others of that caliber. Everybody in Christendom seems to know them and know them so well that they never have to be identified by so much as a last name or a middle initial, let alone a driver's license or a Social Security number! The record of their deeds and sacrifices has been preserved for our edification in the pages of the Scriptures, and from time to time we pause to review the record of one of these great spirits. Yet we recognize that even if every one of the 365 days of the year were earmarked for remembering individual saints, there simply are not enough days to go around, for in addition to those who are identified in the Bible there are many thousands more who are worthy of our attention.

If you have a yen for honor and prestige, then it is only fair to tell you that the best you can aspire to is to be one of God's Saints Anonymous. But, if I may borrow the refrain from an old song, "Who can ask for anything more?" It is a large and good company to be in. It includes those folks in ancient Rome who received a letter from St. Paul in which he greeted them: *"To all God's beloved in Rome, who are called to be saints: Grace to you and peace from God our Father and* the Lord Jesus Christ." It embraces *"the Church of God which is at Corinth, to those sanctified in Christ Jesus, called to be saints together with all those who in every place call on the name of our Lord Jesus Christ, both their Lord and ours." (1 Cor. 1:2)* It unites us with a fellowship that spans the centuries and embraces the whole world.

I am indebted to and grateful for every saint — every child of God — who has played a part in introducing me to the Savior and nourishing me in the faith. I thank God not only for Paul, John and Peter, but also for relatives, pastors, teachers, friends and multitudes of Christ's followers I have never met but who have been God's instruments in quickening and sustaining my faith. Thank you, one and all!

PRAYER:

For all who have shared the goodness of your redeeming love by their words and by their deeds we give you thanks, O Lord. Empower us to follow in their steps. In Jesus' name, Amen.

DISCOVERING MUTUAL TRUST

by Rev. Orville K. Wold

"I often boast about you; I have great pride in you; I am filled with consolation; I am overjoyed in all our affliction."
2 Corinthians 7:4.

One of the great experiences of my life happened in my early teens. A group of my friends and I were enjoying ourselves one summer evening in the city park, sitting on a picnic table, talking. The conversation took a new direction when one of the boys suggested an activity — some tomfoolery that was not acceptable. In a flash, the group took an interest in it! But it troubled me, for it dawned on me that I had some wonderful parents at our house who trusted me and my behavior while I was out of their sight. With some hesitation, I reported my thoughts to my friends. To my surprise, the group took another look at the planned activity and scrubbed their plans.

That incident not only caused me to be very focused on the *trust* others have in me, but it accentuated my appreciation of having parents *I* could trust for my livelihood. Then my thoughts shifted to my appreciation of the trust our Heavenly Father has in us. I had memorized scripture passages that admonish us to Trust The Lord. That was important and became more important as I grew. That mutual trust became and still is the foundation of my life.

It is reassuring to know how totally trustworthy are the promises of God in the scriptures. While still a teenager, I carried the caskets of three of my close friends. The experience was like an interruption in a train of thought, but it was good to be consciously aware that the Triune God could be trusted, even in times like that. Likewise, through threatening illnesses, the accidental death of my father, and other traumatic experiences, it was reassuring to be able to trust God who does not forsake us.

Through all of the attacks on our faith (the doubts which are provoked deliberately, and those which appear just because we are human), God's promises become the Rock that nothing can move, remove, crack or destroy.

Through most of the days of my pastoral ministry, the call process of parish pastor was performed in an amazing trust of process, people and pastor. For the most part, there were no negotiations. The district president was trusted to make recommendations of a pastor who could fit a given parish. The call showed up in the pastor's mailbox without any other conversation. Sometimes, call committees would make a surprise visit on a Sunday morning, but tried to keep a low profile. When the call was delivered, the pastor could accept or return the call. If it was accepted, the pastor would begin work in the new parish with the total trust of the people. What a privilege it was to enjoy that unconditional trust.

PRAYER:

Our Heavenly Father, you trusted our first parents but they broke that trust. You responded by redeeming them and renewing your trust. You have done this through all generations, and we are grateful for it. Because our lives are interjected with temptations to distractions, occasions of broken trust, our lives are steadied by your uninterrupted faithfulness and unconditional trustworthiness. Help us to be more consistent in our trust of you, of one another, and to the limits of all things you have created. Amen.

WHY WERE WE SPARED?

by Rev. J. Philip Worthington

"If it had not been the Lord who was on our side when our enemies attacked us, then they would have swallowed us up alive. Our help is in the name of the Lord, who made heaven and earth." Psalm 124:1-3 and 8 .

In the late summer of 1947, two seminarians were driving at night on the Pan American highway in the mountains north of Mexico City. Suddenly the lights revealed that half of the roadway was not there! A quick swerve brought us onto the remaining half of the road until we found a place to pull off the road and wait for daylight. We learned that half the road was hundreds of feet down the side of the mountain. By the mercy of God, we had escaped death.

How many times has God spared us from death? Recall experiences in your life when death was seconds away and you were spared. Perhaps it was when you were climbing as a child, or when you dozed while driving, or on a battlefield, on a construction job, in an operating room, in flood waters or in the presence of a deranged man with a loaded shotgun. Perhaps it was at a time when you were totally unaware of danger but learned later that you had been spared.

Why do you think we were spared? Ezekiel 18:23 asks whether God has any pleasure in the death of the wicked. Does God not want people to turn from their ways and live? Could it be that we were spared in order that we might repent and live? Or were we spared in order that we might be equipped for a more mature ministry . . . *to the measure of the full stature of Christ?* (Ephesians 4:11-16)

Humbly ponder the question: Why was I spared? Though additional possibilities flow from the Bible, focus on Matthew 28:18-20. Consider the fact that Jesus has been given ALL authority. He commands: *Go . . . make disciples . . . baptize . . . teach . . . and remember, I am with you . . . always.* Can the Great Commission suggest central reasons why we were spared?

PRAYER:

Gracious God, thank you for preserving our lives countless times. Above all, accept our thanks for making us new creations by grace through faith in Christ and for giving us the ministry of reconciliation. Continue, we pray, to spare us until your gracious purposes for us and others are fulfilled. In Jesus' name. Amen.